GOVERNMENT ECONOMICS GONE WILD

BOOKS BY

BENJAMIN ROBERT SILL, JR.

Inflation- Worse than Vampires, Zombies or the
Plague!

Inequality – Must There Be Blood in the Streets!

Government Economics Gone Wild

Downsizing – Efficiency or Greed?

Observations

GOVERNMENT ECONOMICS GONE WILD

Professor Benjamin Robert Sill, Jr. retired

Portions of this book have appeared in other
publications by the author

ISBN 978-0-9972646-4-7 paperback
ISBN 978-0-9972646-5-4- ebook

To my beloved wife, Yasmin, and my wonderful children, Brittany and Parker

ACKNOWLEDGMENTS

Dr. Tom Verney, Dr. Tony Winters and Dr Steve Holoviak at Shippensburg University and, Dr. Karen Frey and Dr. Charles Walton at Gettysburg College for their kindness, support and input, my Doctoral teammates for their support, my students for their youthful energies and survey results, my children, Brittany and Parker, for giving me the incentive to want to leave them with a sense of pride and the urge to succeed; and last but most importantly, my loving wife Yasmin, without whose love, devotion, encouragement and optimistic outlook, this effort would not have been possible and I would have been a shell of a man long, long ago.

Contents

ABSTRACT.. xiii

INTRODUCTION xvii

How Are We Doing.. xviii

Transfer of Wealth to the Rich xxiii

What is the Government's function? xxix

CHAPTER ONE- ATTITUDE................................. 1

Not the Democracy of Ancient Athens. 4

War and Christians 9

Gays and Abortion.. 10

Low Oil Prices.. 12

People (Governments) Do Bad Things................ 18

CHAPTER TWO - HISTORY 19

Rome.. 21

Liberals and Conservatives................................... 24

Governments don't need inflation. 29

The Depression and F.D.R. 31

An Economic Overview from 1996 36

CHAPTER THREE - INFLATION........................ 61

Bubbles.. 63

Deflation.. 64

The Twentieth Century.. 73

Debt 78

Economic Hardship 79

Causes.. 80

Keynesians, Monetarists, and Classicalists 85

CHAPTER FOUR - INEQUALITY........................ 87

Two Worlds Here in America 89

CHAPTER FIVE - WAR.................................... 93

The Siege of Leningrad 99

The Austro-Hungarian Empire 103

Military Industrial Complex 104

CHAPTER SIX - MONEY AND BANKING....... 105

The Creature from Jekyll Island. 116

Fractional Banking System............................... 125

Reserve Currency and Risk Aversion................ 129

Goldman Sachs ~~owns~~ IS the Government 130

Bond pricing and deliberate inflation 136

Real interest rates 137

The velocity of money 138

Inverted yield curve............................... 140

Calculations 142

Goldstone and Fisher Wave Theory................ 143

Gross domestic product (GDP) 146

Marginal Utility................................... 146

Analysis of Money Circulation and Its Sustainability................................... 148

Credit 150

CHAPTER SEVEN - FOREIGN POLICY 153

Saudi Arabia 155

Korea 156

Viet Nam 157

Does the Quran preach violence? 158

Ukraine and Russia 163

Trade Deficits 163

Protectionism 167

CHAPTER EIGHT - BUSINESS PRINCIPALS .. 177

Hyman Minsky 179

Cycles and incompetent implementation 179

Taxes 181

Minimum Wage and Unemployment 187

Housing 190

Welfare 191

The law 192

Education 193

CHAPTER NINE - TECHNOLOGY 195

CHAPTER TEN - IMMIGRATION 203

CHAPTER ELEVEN - COMMENTS 207

Is Greed & Struggle Necessary for Survival 211

Planned Obsolescence 219

Does Capitalism work? 220

Creative Destruction or a Friendly Society? 222

Cowboys and Sheiks.. 225

Sociopaths... 227

Front Running on Insider Information 235

Capitalism versus Communism. 235

   Marx versus Schumpeter................................ 236

Economies require pain 239

Natural Resources.. 241

Social Security is great. 242

This is our fault.. 247

Greece – the worst of the worst......................... 252

A day in the life of a Politician.......................... 256

CHAPTER TWELVE - SOLUTIONS 259

FURTHER RESEARCH 269

APPENDIX A COMPREHENSIVE PLAN TO
BALANCE THE BUDGET.................................. 271

GLOSSSARY 281

REFERENCES 289

ABSTRACT

As prevalent as "Wall Street greed" is, and as nasty and evil as most in the industry are (just like the rest of us), nothing has changed over time. Wall Street is always greedy, only with the means to do something about it. The rich getting more than their fair share is nothing new, it's been going on since the beginning of time. The only thing that might be of interest to us is we are now very near the top of the list of greedy regimes. An important point to note is that even though two wrongs do not make a right, "Greed" has no time boundaries either. It has been going on since the beginning of time: Rome, the Byzantine Empire, England in 1688, India in 1750, Spain in 1752, Mexico in 1790, India in 1801, England in 1801 the Kingdom of Naples in 1811, Brazil in 1872, China in 1880 and India in 1947 (U.S. Bureau of Labor Statistics. , 2015). No doubt there are many more. People — rich and poor — are always greedy. But they don't always have a system put in place for them that encourages debt and favors investors over working people. It was the Federal Reserve and the government who made it possible for the rich to get richer. This system really took off after Nixon took us off the gold standard. It seems to be getting worse with every Federal Reserve chairmen.

Without the requirement for backing by gold after 1971 there was an explosion of credit. Credit is handled by the credit industry (banking and Wall

Street), so they found themselves in a favorable position. The middle and lower classes lose out because they went in debt to buy things. The rich who owned stocks and bonds got richer. Profits in the financial industry quadrupled from 1970 to 2007. Salaries in the financial industry also increased dramatically.

As most institutions mature, they gradually shift from existing to serve their constituents; to manipulation by and self-preservation of those who control them. The people become entrenched and resists any change that would diminish their power and wealth. The process becomes very parasitic and drains resources away from production.

In reading anyone's research, it pays to remember that even with the documentation, it's only someone's subjective opinion. Opinions can be wrong. Use your own good judgment and take everything with a grain of salt. "Everybody who's saying 'buy stocks' today or 'buy real estate' is, I think, setting up people to get really hurt," says Robert Prechter (TSK News, 2009), who believes the bear market rally is reaching a major top." We had a great opportunity when the S&P was at 667" says Prechter. "The market is up 60% and there's no way the S&P is going up 60% from here" (TSK). The market promptly went to 2000, another 100% gain. One of the really scary things about today's economic world is that people like Prechter make perfect sense, yet are still wrong. Opinions can be wrong.

"The outlook for economic recovery is questionable, at best...which means that the outlook for rising share prices is even more questionable," said Joel Bowman in 2010. This for the next time you decide to listen to some financial writing hack. Just one more. It is hard to take a side on the argument about the damage caused to the Russian stocks due to the drop in oil and the sanctions. Will it go back up? Probably, but that doesn't help you if you got in just in time to take the loss.

INTRODUCTION

> "Some writers have so confounded society with government, as to leave little or no distinction between them; whereas they are not only different, but have different origins ... Society is in every state a blessing, but Government, even in its best state, is but a necessary evil; in its worst state, an intolerable one." -- Thomas Paine, Common Sense

How Are We Doing

What kind of a civilization doesn't aspire to improve? Aspiring is certainly a step in the right direction, however, it would also be nice to see some positive results. In order to make a determination, maybe we should revisit some of the numbers and attitudes. Bear in mind that these numbers fluctuate depending on who you ask, but they are all on the right track. We are currently ranked 7th in Literacy, 27th in math, 178th in infant mortality, 22nd in science, 3rd in income, and 49th in Life expectancy. We are 1st in incarceration and defense spending. America is no longer the greatest (Koepka, 2014). If you haven't seen Jeff Daniels' 4 minutes from the series *The Newsroom* on YouTube, you are missing something special.

Our schools stink. Our tax system is confusing and wasteful. College grads can't find decent jobs. Health care is unbelievably expensive. The superrich live in a world far separated from the rest of us. Government officials are on the take and self-serving. Gee, what's not to like?

The U.S. is still No. 1 in two categories— income and housing. The U.S. has the highest average level of household wealth, at $116,000 per household (which isn't income, but assets). Americans also have the highest level of personal earnings: $54,450 per capita (Organization of Economic Cooperation and Development , 2012). Income inequality messes up averages, so basically these figures are hogwash.

Housing affordability in the U.S. ranks eighth out of 36 nations surveyed, while the quality of housing—measured by the portion that have basic facilities such as indoor plumbing—ties for first place with Sweden, Spain and the Netherlands (Organization of Economic Cooperation and Development , 2012). Can you imagine the Spanish being better at anything than say, the Germans or the French or the English? Whether the larger living space we have is necessary is another debate.

We have an exorbitant and ineffective health-care system that costs far more than health-care in any other country at 2.5 times the average for other developed countries - yet life expectancy is still well below average.

As of 2012 the United States ranked 54th in the trustworthiness of its politicians and 76th in the efficient spending of government resources. Most of our politicians are mouthy hypocrites who get nothing done. And in the OECD survey, the U.S. homicide rate ranked a pitiful 32nd out of 36 nations, ahead of only Estonia, Russia, Brazil and Mexico (Organization of Economic Cooperation and Development , 2012)

Guess what groups of baboons- who are loud, aggressive, obnoxious, vicious, dangerous, and the least intelligent of all primates are called? You guessed it, a Congress! That can't be a coincidence.

Too bad we also don't have the tourist trade Europe does, which puts extra money in the coffers and keeps downtown areas alive. The Europeans do have a high VAT (tax), more road taxes and stronger unions. This enables them to have a strong socialistic welfare system, unemployment system and health system. I'm sure there is some bad in there but hey, what the heck? Our government is looking for money right? Send a few note takers over there to see what can be done.

The old cash for clunkers program is a very good illustration of what happens when the government sticks its nose in things. People bought cars when the feds gave them free money. When the money stopped, so did car sales. Sales fell 38% from August to September of that year. It just put tomorrows' sales in today's numbers, leaving tomorrow to languish. Or, conversely, it sometimes pushes bad consequences forward into tomorrow. A prime example is inflating everything in the economy by printing money that is probably never intended to be paid back. That's really tomorrow. The "to be fair" opposing viewpoint would have to be that honest, well-meaning government officials thought it was a good idea to get some money into people's pockets and as a side effect, get some junky cars off the road. Funny, I never got anything because I meant well.

Poor Ben and Janet. I'm so sorry that you don't know what to do. Going to that Ivy League school and all. Must be terrifying. You should have gone to a normal school like most of us. No pressure at all to be right. Of course, we don't get elected to be Chairman of the Federal Reserve either. However, if you don't know what to do, how do you think that makes us feel? The Inflation policy you are pursuing just doesn't look like a good deal for most of us, based on economics 101 from good old Podunk U. Basically this crisis began because there was too much money. Not having enough money has never been an issue. So, tell me again how printing more money is a good thing?

"Keynes would be proud of Bernanke. Both believe that inflation is better than deflation" (Blumen, 2005)

Federal Reserve governors such as Bernanke and Yellen are believers in the 'the zero bound problem (Woodford, 2010), which states that "you can't loan money at less than zero percent interest." There is nothing cheaper beyond "free." It is complicated; which doesn't make it right. In order not to have to lend at less than zero, they propose to create a constant state of "pleasant and benign inflation" of around 2-3%. Who in the world ever came up with that phrase? Why would anyone think that inflation, of any amount, is ever benign, must less pleasant!

I can just picture the scam making the rounds at Washington cocktail parties: "to make money pay a negative nominal interest rate, by imposing some type of 'carry tax' on currency and deposits. That means charge savors to deposit their money." The idea is that you would spend all your money on consumption, rather than saving it, because you would be paying a tax on it if you saved! Seriously, just how much can the higher ups abuse the average person before there is blood in the streets? At some point, there will be nothing left to live for and no reason not to hit the streets. Gees, I don't even care if I'm wrong anymore, that's just not fair.

Then there's Congress. Are they just an embarrassment to themselves for letting this Princeton genius tell them that we can - and will have – constant, simmering inflation, in which, little by little, prices creep upward, but income does not. And every month you have to borrow more money, or give up something, until one day you are rationing basic necessities. Bernanke actually believed in this stupidity.

Ben Bernanke has stated that he believes in the necessity for "unconventional measures" (Blumen, 2005). A series of exotic plans for the dollar. Is that as scary as it sounds? I don't know about you but I would prefer my government not use words like unconventional and exotic.

Do you believe that societies, economies and financial markets are predictable? That's a little presumptuous. But this isn't the way many governmental officials look at it. Based on such a fool hardy assumption they target inflation, economic growth and employment levels to precise decimal places. Their entire premise is that people would be better off spending their money rather than saving it, that prices increases are good, and that, by flooding the market with money so assets will increase, they will cause real growth and prosperity. How stupid is that? I suspect these people also think they are infallible.

Transfer of Wealth to the Rich

In the process the feds have transferred trillions of dollars in unearned wealth to the rich. They increase prices for the middle and lower classes and have created an enormous amount of debt. There is no real economic growth. Who doesn't think the right thing to do when you have too much debt is to pay it down? That's really what was happening in 2008, but the feds interrupted that natural process. Like all liars, after swearing on a stack of bibles to the contrary, eventually the central banks will write off the government debt. Doesn't there have to be a day of reckoning?

Average people probably don't have the time, the money, or the training to be real capitalists, they're busy trying to keep their economic heads above water. This leaves them fair game for the shysters on Wall

Street to cheat. In real terms we have the lowest interest rates in 45 years and the most consumer debt ever.

As of 2010 there were more than 100 million people in some kind of federal welfare program, 64 million on Social Security, 54 million on Medicare and 70 million on Medicaid. Food Stamp recipients stand at 46 million (Durden, 21 Facts That Prove That Government Dependence Is Out Of Control In America, 2014). Even if they are exaggerated, these are horrible numbers and a poor commentary on our way of life. Since it's so easy for the rich and they're so much smarter than the rest of us, why not redistribute and let them start over again? They keep saying how they will have it all back again quickly.

After being in the welfare system or unemployed for a long period of time, it just doesn't matter, the stress has taken its toll. I can't be sure since I wasn't there but I am guessing that the stress levels haven't gotten any better over the last 100-200 years. Granted, times have always been tough for the poor and I would not have wanted to live in mud caked Victorian London or been a cowboy somewhere out West. But aren't we supposed to be improving on all that?

Part of the blame for stress increase may be longer hours with heavier workloads (logical), thanks to downsizing as well as low pay for the sake of an extra nickel for each CEO- not so logical. I just went through a jobs website and 90% of the openings were for educated people and paid only $30-40,000. In 2014 that's not a lot of money. Personalities of the middle managers are not anything to write home about either. No one likes to take know it all orders from some wet behind the ears puppy, but bad communication stinks coming from anyone of any age. Managers are not the only personality deficient employees. Annoying co-workers out to make your life miserable or slit your throat are to be reckoned with. There are fewer opportunities for advancement in a declining economy out for maximum efficiency, constant fear of being fired and fewer chances to choose a career you actually want; consequently there is only a poor work-life balance waiting for you.

It is a slam dunk to say too many companies are making decisions for short-term benefits and not thinking about long-term effects. Clearly that doesn't come from asking some CEO.

It's easy to say that if you lose someone that's valuable to you and you have to start from scratch, there will be significant cost associated with that. Just saying there will be costs associated with it doesn't cure the problem. Why not do something about it? Unfortunately, people generally don't do anything about it thanks to their human frailties.

Nothing is one-sided, however. Workers are no great shakes either. Whether they are miserable because of the work environment or the work environment is bad because of their attitude. Probably a little of both. The lucky ones get to spew dull platitudes such as "find your passion, it's never too late, and enjoy life." Be careful. Don't quit until you have that new job.

Instead of tracking those unemployed-especially since that number has so many flaws in it, why not check the percentage with jobs in the working age category. That number is worse now than 30 years ago. A simple calculation using Social Security numbers shows that half of American workers make less than $30,000. Almost three-quarters make less than $50,000.

The number of people on disability is a joke. Setting aside those who really need help, what about that healthy 6'3" guy who plays touch football on weekends? Any reason to give him a nickel?

It now takes two people working per family to get by. You think this is a well-run government or society?

The thing is, do we say that's a crime because the rich have usurped so much of the pie and our system is broken; or do we say a lot of these people are deadbeats?

Most governments love a good cause, or a good philosophy to push. Although from time to time we hear a lot about how we are the land of opportunity and individualism, there is very little individualism in Washington. Today you are either a Democrat or a Republican, tow the party line and never the twain shall meet. Some believe in the free market system. Some are Monetarists and some are Keynesians. Some are even down right, gosh darn communists. Oh goodness!

The purpose of most elected government officials is to get re-elected, not to help anyone or solve any problems. These guys/gals are not the cream of the crop when it comes to human beings. They may be smart enough but most are flawed with the narcissistic bug, big egos and a craze for power. That can't be a good thing. "Politics favors blowhards, hustlers and shallow opportunists" (Bonner, Poor Ron Paul, 2014).

Frederick Douglass said: "Find out just what people will submit to, and you have found out the exact amount of injustice and wrong which will be imposed upon them ... The limits of tyrants are prescribed by the endurance of those whom they oppress" (Douglas, 2015). In other words, power always corrupts and Government will do whatever it can get away with.

Read this and weep. "The rights of authors, inventors, and innovators are protected by the state. The privacy of citizens, and of their correspondence, telephone conversations, and telegraphic communications is protected by law. No one may, without lawful grounds, enter a home against the will of those residing in it. Respect for the individual and protection of the rights and freedoms of citizens are the duty of all state bodies, public organizations, and officials." What part of our constitution did that come from? The Russian one (Constitution Of The Union Of Soviet Socialist Republics, 1977). Go figure. Do you notice any similarities?

Anyone paying attention should ask, but isn't the government just a bunch of people like you and me? Absolutely. Therein lies the problem. It isn't just a few bad guys, it is the entire structure, and it is very difficult to make corrections. It is almost impossible to fire many of them and there is a lot of money involved. Not a very good combo. No one likes to be proven wrong or critiqued.

Inequality seems to be ingrained in the system. Once you get a foot in the door it's easier and easier to move up. Contacts make the rich get richer. My fear is that we can't help ourselves. The cream rises to the top. Only in this case, the scum rises to the top. It just seems that over   time systems evolve in a certain direction, usually toward corruption. The more you have the more you want. A little power leads to a lust for more power.

Is there a conspiracy in Washington? Heavens no. No one is hiding behind any curtain. It's right there for all to see. I didn't say you weren't getting shafted, just that they make no bones about it. Shame on you for letting it happen.

Safety nets are neat, whether for the poor and unfortunate, or for banks. Actually, more for the poor. The problem is, I don't believe that is mentioned anywhere in the capitalism handbook. You want to use the capitalistic system, then use it. But don't say you are when you protect your buddies and bail out banks. Let's just pick the best of capitalism, and add something for the downtrodden. Nothing for the banks. I tell you what, go ahead and protect the banks, only pay all the scum at the top accordingly, whatever that is. My guess is somewhere around $100,000 per year.

I saw a campaign sign in a yard somewhere. It said the candidate stood for less taxes, more jobs, better education and health care. Well, who wouldn't stand for all that? The trouble is, they never actually accomplish their campaign goals. If you think about it, you can't even accomplish one of those goals without another one suffering. It's hard to have less taxes and more school supplies. Franklin D. Roosevelt was a great example of this. Going into the elections he ran on a platform of balancing the budget. We all know how that turned out, right?

Should Consumer spending drive an economy?

In speaking of government one should have some understanding of the different systems. Did Communism work? It appears to depend on the time frame. 70 years may be too short to make a reasonable decision as to its success or failure. American democracy has lasted for 250 years. Is that a good test time? What about the Greeks? They were finally ousted by barbarians because they were soft. This may not help the logic, except to indicate that in a democracy laziness and debauchery do seem to set in after a while. That doesn't make the barbarians correct either. Lest we forget, capitalism is a predatory market environment - not a good thing I wouldn't think.

What is the Government's function?

Most of us would concede that it is the government's job to go to war- if and when necessary. It is their function to see to the infrastructure and perhaps to care for those in need- the elderly, the disabled and those down on their luck. Not quite so apparent is the job of controlling how the economy operates. Part of that is the right and duty to control corporations, since corporations exist at the pleasure of the state. The government has a moral duty to control excess under its job as a unifier. Everyone needs a system of checks and balances. We have it established by the three part governing among the Judicial, the Legislative and the Executive branch. Why wouldn't that same checks and balances exist in society? I'm not so sure our elected officials read that play book.

If you look carefully you will notice that all trends seem to be getting more volatile. That can't be good, can it? In a 30 year period prior to Nixon closing the gold window the money supply in the U.S. grew less than two fold. In the 30 years since then, the money supply has increased 13 fold. Stock markets have gone crazy as has the real estate market. Plus don't forget that $25,000 low end car that used to cost $700. Must this be a given?

Ten years ago a Korean official used the phrase "structural restructuring." Wouldn't you be embarrassed to say something like that? There is a good chance he is referring to Schumpeter's "creative destruction." How can a government function and assist based on philosophies of destruction? Not that it didn't happen many times. Think Alexander the Great and Napoleon. It's bad enough when some outside force destroys you, but to think your own government has that in mind for you in going to war and creating inflation.

CHAPTER ONE- ATTITUDE

There is no question, that the government, even if well meaning, needs some help.

Public outrage is similar to the government process of sending us into war. Slow and painful if you recognize the signs. First we do some air strikes, then we send a few advisers, then we send some more advisers, then we sent some equipment and finally we send in ground troops. It's always the same. When will we ever learn? Just a lot of talk that doesn't mean anything. We are going to war eventually, and, short of a rare sheer catastrophe, we are not going to change the elite running everything. Every time I open a newspaper (or a web page) all I hear is how mad we are and how we ought to do something about the rich. But it never happens. Short of a French Revolution, that is. Is that the only way to get things done?

Is central banking a cartel, is it good or bad and is it draining the wealth of the middle classes? I think many of us have a short memory as to how things were in the good old days before central banking and democracy. Life wasn't very fair under the "absolute divine right of kings." I don't know what history book you are reading but I don't recall these guys being exactly saints. In fact, usually just the opposite. So, not only no honor among thieves, but among kings either. Plus, if you had the unmitigated gall to die, there was no recourse against your heirs. As always, it was a crap shoot. Sometimes they paid, sometimes they didn't. And when they didn't, lenders went broke. Makes you wonder, what was the Rothschild secret, because that's pretty much how they got rich, right? There are numerous examples, but one classic old world predecessor of modern day Argentina was "deadbeat" King Philip II of Spain. He reneged at least a dozen times. Now, under democracies, the obligations are owed by the nation, not any one individual. In theory that debt also never expires.

In a way this was, and is, a very cleaver but dirty trick. You could say that the individual borrowing the money (congress in our case) has almost no responsibility but gets to spend the money, while people who didn't have a say in the transaction and probably didn't even know it was being borrowed, will have to pay off the debt. Or our children will.

Not the Democracy of Ancient Athens.

Not only does what we call democracy bears no resemblance to that of our forefathers but it doesn't look much like that of the democracy of ancient Athens either. This democracy we know is a relatively recent phenomena, from around the early 1800s. Whether that's meant to be good or bad is left to the reader. With the modern version comes a government owned police department, representatives of the people, not just businessmen or nobles appointed by the King (meaning with a vested interest and beholden for their positions). The whole concept of legislation didn't exist before the time and talents of Jeremy Bentham around 1832. Prior to that the laws were just findings by judges.

If there ever is a wealth tax (as proposed by Thomas Piketty), you can be sure it will somehow be implemented by the rich for the rich. Naturally (ad Hominem), the Republican right feels this is misdirected and doesn't want it. Duh! Piketty goes on to say compliance could be achieved by imposing sanctions if a nation does not comply. (Piketty, 2014) He is on the right track, but admittedly, it would be tough to implement, since international cooperation is not easy to come by. It's the same problem we have with the tax loopholes for corporations and individuals giving up citizenship. Everyone has to be on the same page and that just ain't going to happen.

There is no free market. It **is an exclusive economy.** That's what causes inequality. You can't even play in the game. In fact, my guess is that it gets worse as those with privilege become more entrenched. Front-running stocks through high frequency trading is a great example. The housing market is held up by quantitative easing and low interest rates. The precious metals market is held down by government and Federal Reserve interventions, with the help of the lackey "too big to fail" banks. Low interest rates, another tool of the exclusive, controlled and held down by the Federal Reserve, have enriched the banks, the bankers, Wall Street, borrowers, and speculators at the expense of the savers, the retired seniors, and anyone who doesn't borrow. It is almost impossible to get on the Merry-Go-Round if you are not already there. Property prices have gone ballistic in the upper areas- San Francisco, New York, Miami,

Boston etc. If you don't have property you won't be in a position to ever get property. For one thing, you can't get a loan because you don't have the credit, contacts, and existing money. So the rich get richer.

Worth repeating is the postulation that pure free enterprise may not always be a good thing. In *Road to Serfdom*, Friedrich Hayek insinuates that centralized planning inevitably lead to mass impoverishment and totalitarianism. I will agree there does seem to be a lot of killing in communism; why I haven't figured out yet. That doesn't mean the idea is wrong, just the implementation needs some tuning.

At this stage in a democracy everyone feels they are entitled. The poor want food-stamps, welfare and unemployment comp. The rich want tax cuts, government contracts and insider information. If I were in a kind mood I would say the Fed gets itself in trouble for trying to give to both sides. Mostly they just give to their insider friends while giving lip service to the poor because they need their votes. You don't think they really care, do you?

Granted, we in the United States have exaggerated expectations as to our entitlements. Too many Americans believe their standard of living is a birthright that doesn't have to be earned by hard work. But unfortunately 3 billion people world-wide are now competing with Americans for jobs. It will be hard to fight the onslaught of that many people who want a piece of the pie. By that logic wages will fall until they are comparable. That logic, although possible true, misses the entire point. Not being competitive would be one thing if the rich were not creaming it off the top. So you either protect your industry somehow, or use the cheap labor elsewhere and spread the profits around.

This Foreign Account Tax Compliance Act (FATCA) seems like a great example of something; either a fine example of hubris, or a cocky arrogant government, or simply something to be avoided, focusing on words like "extraterritorial jurisdiction" and "imperial overreach". Not touchy feely words.

I am always amazed at how some people think they are better than everyone else. No question there are those less fortunate who were not blessed with high intellect. Others haven't had the environmental advantages. Just remember, if you were blessed, that many of your brethren believe in Noblesse Oblige and you might want to consider it also. Whenever I read about someone like Zbigniew Brzezinski saying things in his book like "Such a society will be dominated by an elite, unrestrained by traditional values", my skin starts to crawl a little.

But you can bet the second the opportunity presents itself- meaning tight labor conditions, the employees will act with equal greed, trying to squeeze every nickel he/she can. It is human nature, and not very flattering. Even Wall Street was only getting what they could- it was the governments fault for offering. As discussed above, Wall Street is smarter than the government, knows it and doesn't let anyone forget it.

Want to know just how screwed up your government and society are? Here's a little jewel on what's going on here in the United States. With all the hoopla about Islam being or not being an aggressive religion, Christianity has received a bye with the assumption that Christ preached kindness, turn the other cheek, and did unto others etc. There really isn't a lot of kill thy enemies coming from Jesus. So it seems somewhat ironic that both Christianity and the Military Industrial complex are platform staples for the Republican right. The righteous right. The third wing of this unholy alliance is athletics, which has always been a bit too close to a military like attitude. No room for number two and don't want to be number two. Put them all together and you have any opening ceremony today. God Bless America while a wounded veteran stands by with a flag while we sing some war like song. Sounds just like Nazi Germany to me. It's a good thing I'm not running for any office because it is also a fact that a vast majority of Americans believe in this clap trap, so not so many votes for ol' Bob. Even our reasons for going to war are now some kind of "spread the word and make the world safe for Democracy and God. Well, I guess that hasn't changed too much.

All of this so General So and So, a guy who couldn't make it on the outside, can have a place to go and play soldier and the military industrial complex can sell some more weapons. Oh, and we can pay outrageous sums of our hard earned money to a new breed of killer- the private armies that remind you of some cyborg-robot theme combined with pinned stripped CEOs- all with money falling out of their pockets and mean as hell, ready to kill anything that moves with their bare hands. Remember, it isn't the fault of the foot soldier who comes home crippled or in a body bag, even though there is a preponderance of southern good ol boys and blacks serving, it's the fault of greedy, stupid, selfish, unfeeling people in control with a bully mentality combined with a lust for money.

War is not good, it's not glorious, it's not a way out of recession and it's not productive; and anyone with any feeling, brains or maturity knows this. But if you denounce this game in any way they insinuate that you're a traitor. You know, "if you're not with me, you're against me."

Now our police have become just like the military, not that they were saints before. Now they're uneducated, prejudiced, stupid, mean and have automatic weapons.

War and Christians

Then there's the "Imaginary", either God or enemy. In the case of the enemy, if you ain't got one, invent one. The idea is to keep the American people scared out of their minds of an "immediate threat" necessitating an immediate protective response. What hogwash. Other than the far- fetched reasoning advanced by a former movie theater employee in a hoodie that there are a bunch (thousands) of mean guys (young Middle Eastern Jihadists) here already that will somehow causes immense damage, did you ever ask yourself just how would ISIS pose an immediate threat to us without an Air force or Navy? Clear and Present

Danger I suppose. Again, H.L. Mencken also said it years ago, "The whole aim of practical politics is to keep the populace alarmed (and hence clamorous to be led to safety) by menacing it with an endless series of hobgoblins, all of them imaginary."

Don't forget, the mutually exclusive expression is "War Christian".

Speaking of Democracy, and our wish to "spread it" throughout the world, Bagdad in 2014 was having some fun with "elections". They think democracy means majority rules, so Shiites are OK with that (they're the majority), but that doesn't mean they will treat everyone equal, politically or otherwise. Maybe there is something to that Benevolent Dictator thing.

Gays and Abortion

What the hell is my government doing passing judgment on gays? So they can't procreate, that's why it is a genetic anomaly and out of the norm. That doesn't mean you have to procreate, just that you can. Is there a biological propensity to be gay? Seems so. Does it have to do with how your mother treated you? Gays seem to be slightly harder working than the average slovenly heterosexual, they have a great design flair, and are not as prone to violence. Of course, neither are Marijuana users if they don't go on to harder drugs. I think we're on to something.

Abortion falls under this flag also. How tough is this? It's someone's private personal body. Who in the world would ever think they had a say in that? Well, your government, as well as a bunch of right wing, do gooder, religious fanatics, that's who. Fix bayonets! Who the hell thinks they have a right to interfere in a woman's personal intimate body affairs?

So what is the government's function? Last I heard it was to protect its citizens (not wage war on their behalf), create and care for infrastructure (roads and bridges), see that citizens treat each other fairly and nicely and that's about it. That all sounded great back in 1776. Funny how things take on a life of their own and get out of hand.

There is a game theory roaming around that may have bearing on my "human nature" effect. It's called the Prisoner's dilemma. You and a friend get busted for drugs. If you keep your mouths shut, you will both walk away. But if one of you rats out the other, the snitch will go free and the other will do time. If you both turn on each other, both of you will do time. Applying that to our daily business and personal lives; are you nice to the people you deal with? Or do you look out for No. 1, regardless of the consequences to others? A reasonable plan would be to open the game with kindness and generosity. If that nice move is countered with a nasty move, retaliate with equal cruelty and cunning. Every once in a while we turn the other cheek.

A major and serious part of our dilemma is the consumptive, not productive attitude. Our entire corporate and social culture is based around current gratification. Very few people or corporations are willing to delay consumption and save or invest.

Low Oil Prices

Here's another conjured up dilemma. Low oil prices undermine oil-exporting economies (and the American shale industry). Many of the oil producers buy off their lemmings and any potential instability with token bread and water (actually quite a bit of welfare gifts) using oil revenue. If the price of oil goes down that becomes more difficult. From a foreign policy standpoint so what? Why not let them kill each other? Low prices also increase unemployment and reduce capital spending in the oil industry in places like the U.S., Canada and Mexico. See, politicians and economists will have an excuse for everything. You can't win. I have no doubt the part about buying off their population is true, though who is more to blame is up for grabs. Are the people unemployed because they are lazy and want to be, or because most all the wealth is being hoarded by the oil sheiks? I can't imagine what your complaint is if things are cheaper for you. For those companies reliant on high oil prices, it just goes to show their interests are not yours and secondly, simply lower the costs you pay to reflect the new lower prices. That goes for the American Shale Industry also. It makes you want to vomit. Moaning about oil now being too cheap! Make up your mind. I never realized just how unreliable and irresponsible news letters were until this recent downtrend in oil. These guys will say anything to sell you something.

JP-Morgan Chase estimated that, as of December 2014, if oil prices stay low, 40% of all high-yield energy bonds could default (Hamid, 2014). The question is, so what? The investors rode the wave up, why not lose their money- much of which is recent profit anyway. The economy did not collapse with the market at 7000, why would it this time? Looking back, that didn't happen, did it?

In 2012 the Paris-based International Energy Agency (IEA) reported that the United States is set to overtake Saudi Arabia and Russia as the world's top oil producer by 2017. This is due to fracturing and horizontal-drilling techniques ("fracking") that unlock "tight oil" and shale gas resources (Fraser, 2012).

Estimates of the United States' oil shale reserves put it ahead of Saudi Arabia and Russia. The estimates are all over the board but generally put 2013 production at 10.9 million barrels per day. In a decade, shale gas has risen from 2% of U.S. natural gas production to 37% (Perkins, 2013). Even though the figures don't jive, are short lived or exaggerated there is good evidence that shale oil and gas has helped the American economy by reducing costs.

The oil and gas drilling boom has created millions of jobs. And these are high paying jobs, not fast food or health-care jobs. Taxes on high salaries help the government as well. Corporate costs go down also.

It would be such a relief to not be under the threat of blackmail by OPEC, because they proved in the 1970s that they would destroy us if they could.

If the oil and gas boom were to continue, our foreign policy will focus much less on the Middle East where it must cost a fortune to maintain fleets of aircraft carriers and why would we do that for China and India, who will be now buying most of the oil?

On the other hand, there are concerns. These wells do not produce nearly as much oil as a Middle Eastern one and the depletion rates are much faster.

If you are a believer in and supporter of the Supply and Demand Theory then the more they pump, the lower prices go, which would not be in their best interest. Better to cut production and get more money for less production. Hard to fight that logic. Now another theory has taken shape. OPEC believes, or so it seems, that cheaper oil prices will put pressure on high-cost US shale-oil producers. This is a long term calculated risk although the Saudis have little to lose.

The naysayers say new wells will not be drilled, no one will try solar panels, no one will buy electric cars, and as soon as all that happens, OPEC will again raise the price of their oil. Bull. Don't kid yourself, low prices are a good thing.

Sean Brodick forecast $200 per barrel in 2008, (Brodick, 2008). Andrew Mickey forecast $30 oil way back in 2007 (Mickey, 2007). You know it doesn't count if it happens 10 years later, right? So, they are either liars or simply don't know what will happen. (Maybe they are just exaggerating in order to sell financial newsletters.) The point is, take everything you read with a grain of salt. Even in this piece you find glaring errors. Following is a great example: According to Citigroup, the fiscal break-even cost – the price governments need oil to stay above to meet their spending commitments is: $161 for Venezuela, $160 for Yemen, $132 for Algeria, $131 for Iran, $126 for Nigeria, $125 for Bahrain, $111 for Iraq, $105 for Russia, and $98 for Saudi Arabia (Lowe, 2014). Totally misleading! The key word is spending commitments. That means it includes the expense of running their countries, not just the cost to produce. The Saudis costs are actually just $2 a barrel (Davidson, 2012). So in late 2014 with oil at $52/barrel they are losing money? The confusion here lies in the word profitable. When the Middle East speaks of profit they mean after paying all their social welfare programs. Not really the same. Abdalla El-Badri, OPEC's secretary-general, said that half of all US shale output is unprofitable below an oil price of $85 a barrel. All US shale-oil producers aren't as vulnerable to $70 dollar oil as OPEC claims. Parts of the Bakken formation are profitable at $42 a barrel. In McKenzie County, the most productive county in North Dakota, the break-even cost price is $28 (Davidson).

Government officials should have a handle on these numbers and the truth to them if any. Sadly, governments and economies do rely still and for a long time on fossil fuels.

Although there is little doubt that oil is a critical commodity and the supply of it is mostly in the hands of those who can least handle it best, or certainly are not handling it in our interests- not exactly the same. Nevertheless, by at least one report (Masters Capital Management), speculation does also have an effect on oil prices.

Is there such a thing as Peak Oil? Why wouldn't there be? If you are growing corn you can grow some more next season. Even trees can be grown in twenty years or so. It takes millions of years for oil to form, so yes, it can run out.

Americans each use 25 barrels of oil per year. The Chinese each use 2 barrels of oil per year. And Indians each use 1 barrel of oil per year (IndexMundi, 2014). Call it foreign policy, or economics or self-preservation. These other countries are going to want to have what we have and will!

Why are we so pig headed regarding drilling in Alaska and off the coast of California and Florida? Why does it take so long to build a refinery? Are there enough ships to transport the oil and enough drilling rigs to get the job done? Why has the price of a drilling ship gone from $150,000 to $600,000 per day? To hear the oil cry-babies whine, everything would be just fine if they were allowed to drill on Federal Land. Well, sort of. Granted there is probably oil on off limits Federal land, but there's plenty also on 68 million acres of land that oil companies can currently drill, but aren't. Over a recent four year period 10,000 more permits were issued to oil and gas drillers than were used. That means the companies are actually stockpiling extra permits. For those of you who are enamored with

Capitalism and the "free market system", this is what you get. In the Gulf of Mexico only around 25% of the leases are in production. Does the reason they are not drilling matter?

Don't forget, due to out burdensome policies and processes it takes years to get anything done so why not begin everything now? I suspect the Democrats are on the wrong side of this issue. But GOP members of the Senate put the kibosh on a bill that would have extended tax credits for wind power, solar, and renewable energy sources like biomass, geothermal, landfill gas and trash combustion. There is no good excuse for the GOP action except they are in the pockets of big oil.

Should we continue to conserve? Absolutely. Every little bit helps. Just like the alternative situation. Maybe one alone won't cure our ills but a little wind, solar, geothermal bio-fuels and conserving would go a long way. Don't believe all the hype dribbled out by the environmentalists. Same things goes. Sure, you must be careful not to cause damage. Tell that to the chemical industry also.

Let's split the difference with regulation and tax breaks. Reasonable regulation and no tax breaks.

Comparing the foreign policy between China and the United States, let's see, they go out and make deals while we makes enemies. By the way, as asked elsewhere, tell me again what our plan was in Iraq? To get some oil? That went well, huh?

I would poo-poo the Apocalyptic literature on the Middle East, oil and the biblical references except

I notice all the Vampire movies on the TV. I wonder how much of the garbage will be self-fulfilling?

People (Governments) Do Bad Things

We live with a government that believes it is perfectly OK to put a person's life in harm's way simply because her husband disagreed with them. If you speak with Karl Rove or others like him he would tell you they have done nothing wrong, it's just politics as usual.

And yet, just who is it that does all these either bad or stupid things? We say it's our government. But isn't the government made up of people like us? The only answer I can think of is, no, they're not. You know, all humans are evil, just some are more evil than others. This Military Industrial thing must really be a force to be reckoned with, and the people in it total jerks. It just occurred to me (for the 10th time) that we had another phenomenal opportunity at the end of the cold war to clean up our act and strengthen our economy. Without the Soviets nipping at our heels we could have saved a bundle by reducing the military budget significantly. We didn't. We armed even more, became more of a bully and adapted Keynesian economics. Talk about a death wish. I would truly enjoy hearing the other side's justification for all that, I just don't have enough candy bars and cokes stored up. Besides that, in a little over two decades Russia has come roaring back stronger than ever.

CHAPTER TWO - HISTORY

What's that expression? "Those who fail to learn from history are doomed to repeat it." Why, after several thousand years, can't we get our acts together? It isn't as though we haven't had chances. If you're trying to stay in power, and do a good job (somewhat mutually exclusive tasks), you would think you would be a student of histories' mistakes.

It is also important to remember, "History is written by the winners." Whatever is left over is written by governments, who pay for the books. It makes governments look good and winners blameless and good guys. This is done because you have to justify your previous actions and continue conning the people into believing they must serve their government, and anything else would be treasonous. Anytime you can lie like a rug and make the people believe you, especially if you can somehow make them believe they are special in the process, you have earned the government merit badge

Rome

I don't know what happened in earlier civilizations but look no further than the great Roman Empire for your first lessons. Becoming a decedent society with declining moral values, losing political civility at home, an overconfident and overextended military in foreign lands, and fiscal irresponsibility by the central government.' "The Roman Empire existed on tribute obtained by brute force. Spending too much money on military operations and debasing the currency didn't go too well for them. Sound familiar? So, as a government, mind your own business militarily and balance your budget. How tough is that? That doesn't even begin to address the kindness issue versus the brute force thing. On the military deal, take a look at Switzerland to see what good can come of minding your own business.

As to the budget, there are scores of examples of money printing for guidance. Paper money was first issued in the new world by the French Military in Canada, in 1685 (Encyclopedia Britannica, 2015). Quick and dirty, no problem as long as it is backed by solid assets and convertible into those assets. In other words, don't exceed your collateral. The solid asset can't be future earnings or taxes either, they're not guaranteed. Also, try not to print 100% of the collateral. Maybe 80% of the asset?

How come no inflation today from the excess printing? Simple, because the printed money isn't getting into the economy. The banks are hoarding it or it is going to the rich.

Any self-respecting Austrian School sound money economist knows the story of John Law in France in the 1700s. Same story- more money printed than there was backing for it.

For the layman among us, if the money supply goes up prices will come down. I didn't say you had to agree with it, or that it was consistent with what's happening today.

Probably wouldn't hurt to have that same working knowledge of Marx, whether you believe what he said or not. Maybe even a willingness to debate the philosophical differences between The Austrian School and our beloved John Maynard Keynes.

Most any war will necessitate going into debt. That doesn't address the larger issue of why you went to war in the first place. Remember, even Keynes understood the need to pay back the debt. Oops.

The government must come up with some way to control the Bank temptation not to destroy money being paid off and reissuing it instead. If the whole purpose of printing money is for the convenience of commerce, then it is a substitute for the hard asset (gold). That means you can't have both in the economy at the same time. The government may want to revisit the entire Fractional banking theory also.

It is oftentimes used as an excuse that the government has to suspend convertibility (think Nixon) because there is too much of a demand for the gold. How can that be if the printed money was always backed by the gold? If the gold were being redeemed someone had to have spent currency somewhere on something for said party to obtain of the money (to use for redemption) in the first place.

Is it just me or does there seem to be no problems when your currency is backed by gold, or something!

All the major players in the 1700s took a whack at the problem; Ricardo, Adam Smith, Bosanquet, etc.

In fact, it probably would serve us all well to understand who stood for what and when at little. To do that it may help to know what these ideologues thought (think) they stand for.

Liberals and Conservatives

Called Liberals/Labor/Whigs depending on the time frame, as led by William Gladstone in the 1800s, they stood for peaceful international negotiations. Gladstone said, "You don't love war, it isn't heroic and it isn't good for the economy as it misdirects resources and destroys them." (Powell, 1996) He knew that the war was costly and that alone should be a major deterrent. Gladstone and his party believed in reform, state's rights, local rule, and small Federal government. Gladstone believed in free discourse, the free exchange of ideas, tolerance of other points of view (without necessarily approving of those views), freedom to pursue happiness, health, occupation, free trade, less taxation, freedom of religion, constitutional principles of government, laissez faire economics, and noblesse oblige (those who have it should be obligated to help those less fortunate) (Powell) Freedom yes, but with responsibility.

Conservatives/Tories- Led by Benjamin Disraeli who was an imperialist- A real puzzler because he was for the aristocracy as well as the working man and trade unions. He was a protectionist.

Modern Liberals believe in more government, more spending on welfare, more taxation for the redistribution of wealth and possible a one world order. Today's Liberals scorn religion for secular life. One would have to judge for themselves whether they are a government caring for its people, or a government sticking its nose in where it doesn't belong. They have sort of an Animal Farm equality: All animals are equal, just some more equal, particularly themselves as the elite.

Modern Conservatives – are generally far right religious fanatics, believing in more spending on war, and favoring the rich. They can't seem to get along and don't seem to want to. Their claim is to espouse a balanced budgets, but don't really. They do espouse a truly free society and capitalism- which of course, really isn't; it's crony capitalism (that when you want to socialize losses after pocketing profits). No level playing field.

So, initially Liberals were for freedom and conservatives were for governmental controls, which has reversed except conservative freedom is cronyism freedom; conservatives were for the aristocracy and still are for the rich and powerful. The liberals today say they are for the little guy but they are elitists, somewhat like old conservatives.

Aristotle said, "The greatest pleasure a free man could possess is to have the economic means to indulge himself in the study of nature, books, science (philosophy) and the liberal arts, rather than to be forced to labor endlessly with no free time for leisure and the contemplation of life. He was a classic liberal. Outstanding, except someone has to do the grunt work! Your government has decided on you for that task.

A President, according to Classical Liberalism, is mostly a figurehead and a symbol. He can't tax, go to war, create entitlements for either the rich or the poor, can't stick his or her nose into private lives, regulate schools, spy on people, can't have a central bank that inflates the money supply and brings on business cycles, or change the laws to suit the special interests. All this guy should do is play nursemaid to a very small government, arbitrate disputes among the states. His position is actually inferior in importance to those other statesmen on local levels. He obeys the laws and doesn't forget he serves at the pleasure of the people and will be booted out if he crosses them.

This president would also be a man of outstanding character. That's a good one. Where are we going to get one of those? One of the problems we have in this country is our hero worship. We do it with movie stars, athletes, CEOs, and politicians. Why not the President? He's just a guy (or gal) who ought to bow down and be grateful for the position. Richard Nixon was a crook, Clinton was a whore monger, Bush II was something less than an Einstein. But to hear people talk about them, they were Gods.

As we yearn for the "good old days", we must remember that it wasn't all peaches and cream, even then.   States had the right to secession. Private associations dominated social life. Religion was more influential. Also that kind of government would not have made room for things like the Americans with Disabilities Act. That kind of government dictated how to build buildings, who you could hire and how much to pay, regardless of other people's abilities. Don't forget the bevy of "can't be fired" bureaucrats and get rich quick lawyers who specialize in manipulating the system. To be fair, it was not because they didn't like handicapped people or thought that people should be discriminated for or against. They just felt the government should keep its nose out of your business.

Thomas Jefferson understood and wrote that "Men are to be bound from mischief with the chains of the Constitution" (Jefferson, 1798). Virtually none of can be trusted if the prize is big enough so we need restraints. You have to have rules. Or as Madison said in the Federalist Papers, "All men having power ought to be distrusted to a certain degree" (Madison, 1787). And a government employing so many people, most of them armed to the teeth, ought to be distrusted a lot. A true statement which doesn't address the extremes necessary to "have the right to do your own thing".

Classic Liberalism was countered by absolutism. Led by Jean Jacques Rousseau whose view was that "a democratic government embodied the general will of the people, this will was always right, and therefore government would always be right and should have absolute, centralized power over a militarized and unified egalitarian nation-state. Rousseau's theory found followers in Marx and Keynes, They allege that society cannot run itself; instead the general will, the interests of the proletariat, or the economic plans of the people need to be organized and embodied in the nation and its head" (Fehér, 1990). Smart people think dumb things. The question to ask is why? So true how the "best laid plans of mice and men" go astray

There is always some reason for the government to take away some of your rights, the Cold War, the Second World War, the Depression, the First World War. If there isn't one you can be sure your government will create one. Government has no power and no resources that it doesn't first take from the people.

Now the Republicans are spenders just like the Democrats. Both sides say reduce government, balance the budget, decrease the deficit, and lower taxes. How is that done?

Ludwig von Mises advocated private property ownership and its control for everyone. If the government can only work with resources it takes from others, and if all resources are owned and controlled by private parties, the government is restricted and can't seize power, as in wars, depressions, and natural disasters. There can be no exceptions. Remember that pendulum though. If you buy into that, then the TVA (Tennessee Valley Association) would not have built, no one gets bailed out in a natural catastrophe, there would be no war on poverty and no bank bailouts. Some good, some bad, see? Also, the freedom to do as you please, work for and with whomever you please sounds great until things become too skewed and the gap in wealth widens too much. Again, tough business this economics. Mises insinuated that this kept peace. Not so sure. Anti-discrimination laws would not be consistent with the Classic Liberalism. Are they right or wrong? Or is it more complicated? No association that is forced can ever be good for the parties involved or society at large, said Mises. Many of these brilliant 18th century thinkers thought equality was over-rated also and unattainable., even nonsensical. Mises felt human nature couldn't handle equality (right but needs to be addressed), so "the best society can do for its members is to establish rules that apply across the board." There's the rub! Agreed! At least that would be a start! Why should the very rich always be with us? There are those (not counting the CEOs) who believe it is the job of charity, not government, to care for the poor. Who's to say this is right or wrong? There is also the question of protecting individuals from themselves. Tough call.

Opposition came in both Europe and America from the likes of the ACLU who claimed there must be some way for both civil liberties and socialism to co-exist.

Governments don't need inflation.

Looks like global trade does have an effect on inflation. From 1871 to 1948 (excluding the World War years), the transcontinental railroad and the Suez Canal came into being, which expanded global and intercontinental trade. Efficiency ruled the day so prices were contained (Hardcastle, 1990).

How come? Because governments before 1914 knew how to stabilize prices. If currency is increased prices will go up and if reduced, prices will go down..

They knew that the key to the situation is the amount of currency in circulation. If this is kept in line with the needs of the growth of production, population, etc. prices will be stabilized. I guess today's politicians and economists didn't do their homework. Or is it possible they just don't want currency to be stable?

Before 1914 stability was maintained through the gold standard which closely controlled the issue of currency by the Bank of England. In 1920-25 the currency in circulation was cut by burning £66 million worth of notes.

For many years I put Theodore Roosevelt on a pedestal. He was one of my idols. After all, his face is carved into Mount Rushmore, right? For the most part he was even handed in politics, being fair with both parties. His actions suggested that he was for equal rights in regards to blacks. Here was a man who wanted to help the common man, to improve worker conditions and give them decent pay.

On closer inspection we find a throwback to absolutism and the likes of Disraeli, Queen Victoria, any number of Kings, and many of the well thought of liberals and conservatives in the 19th century. To have a sense of Noblesse Oblige, I suspect you believe yourself to be noble and better than others. Blue bloods. It's real easy when you don't have to worry about money.

But that's not the worst of it. In reality, the guy was nothing but a bully with a cowboy attitude; an egomaniac who used words like "bully", "was great fun"(war), "had a brisk fight", "Supreme triumph of war better than any in peace", and the books he wrote were filled with I, I, I, Me, Me, Me. He was an imperialist and needed to show his manhood. A vain glory hound, desperate to get into battle who once said "we need a war". He was itching for one and any excuse would do. He loved the idea of war and believed might makes right. In the fiasco that made him a household word in Cuba, he all but fomented the war, didn't listen to his superiors, was totally out of line in that stupid charge up San Juan Hill and later made the remark that he would have left his wife's deathbed to fight.

He was too rigid- too by the book (he closed the bars on Sunday due to some archaic law on the books.) If he hadn't been rich and pushy, he would have been thought of as the Mr. Milquetoast in the office with pursed lips tapping his watch while watching you get ready to leave at 5:0'clock. No doubt he was a bit deranged, with demons- a functioning neurotic, like a 6 year old on steroids.

The Depression and F.D.R.

Dr. Bernanke accepts Milton Friedman's theory of the Great Depression, which states that a contraction of the money supply turned what would have been an ordinary recession into the Great Depression. This catastrophe could have been avoided, says Bernanke and Friedman, had the Fed inflated sufficiently." Their philosophy is, make so much money available, at such low interest rates, that people can't stop themselves from borrowing and spending, which will jump start the economy. There is certainly no limit to the amount of debt that people will carry, but can they carry it? I love it. Ever-increasing asset values? Sign me up. Of course there is a limit. When the interest you owe is more than your entire income, you're done for.

"The real roots of the 1930s bust were in the 1920s boom. That's when the Fed gave cheap money to the banks like there was no tomorrow. That's why the banks loaned the money to the brokers, the brokers loaned it to speculators, and the speculation created the stock market bubble. That was the true cause of the Crash and the Depression! Not the government's 'inaction' in the 1930s! (Weiss, The Ultimate Depression Survival Guide, 2009)

Murray Rothbard in his book, *America's Great Depression,* looked at the Fed's inflationary actions during the 1920s and estimated that the Federal Reserve expanded the money supply by more than 60 percent from mid-1921 to mid-1929. (Rothbard, 1963). Enter the flood of easy money, low interest rates, the stock market "bubble" and the "Roaring Twenties."

So all the Fed was really doing in 1929 was trying to get back to ground zero. It did exactly what it was supposed to do; cut off the money supply and raised interest rates. Classic boom and bust. Are we learning anything yet?

Franklin Roosevelt didn't think Hoover really practice a "hands off the economy," free-market philosophy? Roosevelt blasted Hoover for spending and taxing too much, boosting the national debt, choking off trade, and putting millions of people out of work. He said Hoover was "reckless and extravagant," and of thinking "that we ought to center control of everything in Washington as rapidly as possible." The only question would be if true, why continue with the same policies? Which he immediately did. His platform said, "We believe that a party platform is a covenant with the people to be faithfully kept by the party entrusted with power." It called for a 25 percent reduction in federal spending, a balanced federal budget, a sound gold currency, the removal of government from areas that belonged more appropriately to private enterprise, and an end to the "extravagance" of Hoover's farm programs. (Roosevelt, 1938)I guess the lesson to be learned here for you politicians is lie through your teeth.

The Roosevelt administration did it again by creating expensive agencies financed by taxes on the very manufacturing industries they were forcing into cartel like arrangement through fascist-style rules. Estimates say this ran up the cost of doing business 40%.

A lot of time should be spent revisiting protectionism also. It definitely got a bad rap in the 1930s due to the Smoot-Hawley Act, which appeared to stifle world trade- a bad thing supposedly. The consensus was, and is, that raising trade barriers will force Americans to buy more goods made at home, which would solve the production and unemployment problems. The other side says trade is a two-way street and if foreigners cannot sell their goods to us, then they cannot earn the dollars they need to buy from us. But we don't sell that much overseas! Another time, another place.

Politicians should be cognizant of the good and the bad provided by the labor unions. How can the Germans make it work so well?

Lastly, for this era, war does not cure anything. Do the math.

The point here is not to instantly determine what is right or what is wrong, just take a look and reflect. Even Irving Fisher made a mistake late in 1928 with his prediction of permanently high stock market prices

Lots of nice things happened in the early 1900s. Electricity, mass production, better farming practices. Is there a lesson in there for a government to encourage innovation?

History has told us that when inflation's limit is reached, it always ends badly. Tell that to Janet Yellen?

One of the finest men to occupy the White House was thought to be one of the worst- Jimmy Carter. During the Carter years the nation was at peace, with the exception of the Iran Crisis in 1979 when they took 52 hostages from our embassy and kept them for over a year. (U.S.State Department, 2015) Despite inflation, Americans were still getting richer. Wages were rising. We still enjoyed a positive balance of trade, and the rest of the world still owed us more than we owed. But in 1980, stocks had been going down for 14 years and bonds had been in a bear market that began in 1945. Maybe that is the way it should be. Nobody ever said markets are to go up always. The Vietnam War was still in the near background. So was Richard Nixon. Plus ol' Jimmy Carter himself. But you know us Americans, never satisfied.

Then, along came Ronald Reagan with a message of hope, optimism, and something-for-nothing. The supply-side, the Laffer Curve! Suddenly it seemed possible to spend more... and still have more! Government could cut taxes - and get more revenue, said Laffer. Forget the deficit; it will take care of itself. Somehow. The average man figured he could do the same: borrow more, spend more, and he would get rich. The Reagan Era also came with a relatively new idea, that people should be responsible for their own pension. Free people could look out for themselves. They could set up their own 401(k) plans and make money in common stocks. Because they thought themselves smart enough. Wrong! Supply-side policies never really increased the supply side. Companies stopped offering fixed (defined) benefit pension plans. We went to defined payment plans. By 2000, old people were feeling the effects. They were not as well off as they had expected to be. When the smoke cleared, near-retirees turned out to be a little poorer, in constant dollars, than the previous generation was when it approached retirement in 1983. Why do we put these people on a pedestal like Reagan, Kennedy, Teddy Roosevelt. Carter was a nuclear Physicist. Reagan was a B actor. Kennedy was just rich, but his Daddy was a bootlegger and sold to the

Third Reich. Theodore Roosevelt was just a war mongering bully.

An Economic Overview from 1996

Not only is it interesting but informative to browse the past for signs you can use to judge the present. Even a short twenty year time span may hold some useful information so this small segment reaches back in time to see what if anything has changed.

Throughout history economic swings have alternatively destroyed lives or dramatically improved our well-being. During the past five years or so it has been particularly unsettling to those of us who thought the United States was invincible and our living standards would continue to rise. From our inception as a nation and especially since the dawn of the Industrial Revolution, the U.S. has been a land of opportunity, filled with hope and enthusiasm. Our living standard has consistently improved even as business cycles rose and fell and recessions have come and gone. In the late 1800'S we were busy opening up new land masses. Although sometimes difficult, the opportunity was there for anyone who wished to work. In the "Gay nineties and steadily through the roaring 20's we prospered and partied. We had stable prices, low unemployment, increasing productivity and economic growth. Easy money policies were followed, taxes were reduced and the government ran surpluses. The theory at the time was classic, i.e., free markets tend toward full employment.

Certainly not everyone was a recipient of the good life but gradually all levels improved.

So, what happened? How could the good times go bad so fast? The answer can be found in several different areas. The passage of the Smoot-Hawley Act is generally regarded as a high ranking offender. School is still out on that, mind you. The ugly head of protectionism created a downward spiral as countries attempted to get even via more and more restrictions, less and less goods got sold and confidence eroded more and more. Shattered confidence is hard to turn around and fear of loss led inevitably to a run on the banks. Inadequate government policies could not stem the tide. GNP declined, Industrial production fell and Wholesale prices fell. Unemployment during the 1930's was high. Finally, bad weather, lack of credit and the low confidence level lead to the creation of the "Dust Bowl" era.

The stage was set for a timely introduction of Keynesian Economics. It was felt during the 1930's that inadequate aggregate demand was the culprit and Franklin Delano Roosevelt (FDR) primed the pump through his many "New Deal" measures. Although a really innovative idea at the time, to this day the concept has yet to be proven valid. Even in the late 1930's, the idea hadn't really caught on and we were still not doing well. It took a war to create a need for production and, more importantly I believe, change our attitudes. We were busy producing guns, tanks, and airplanes. Unemployment dropped dramatically because everyone was being paid to fight a war. However, there was also a correspondingly huge increase in the federal budget and the budget deficit. We began to see significant increases in income taxes, and inflation reared its ugly head. Why not just manufacture something other than guns and tanks and not bother to kill people? **Why didn't FDR's projects work, when a war did?**

After the war the expansion took off like a rocket. Why wouldn't it with such compelling reasons-pent up demand for goods and services, lots of savings, expanded plants and equipment, the baby boom, the Marshall Plan, the G.I. Bill and new industries (aeronautics, electronics and data processing). With such a cushion we could hardly go wrong. We didn't. During the 1950's the United States had steady growth in GNP and personal incomes. Prices were stable with wholesale prices increasing around 1.6% and consumer prices about the same. The recessions were mild and the money supply growth rate was less than 2%. Deficits were small and not constant. It was during this time that we saw the emergence of the Modern Quantity Theory of Money linking price levels with the money supply.

On the surface this happy time continued into the 1960's. From 1961-1969 we experienced the longest expansion in U.S. history to date. Inflation was modest at under 2% until 1965 and from then until 1970 still under 5%. Somehow it is hard to believe those figures with all the money we were spending in Viet Nam. Underneath it all, in fact, a few problems were lurking. That war; one from which we may never recover, changed forever our attitudes about not only war but about ourselves. Authority was held up to scrutiny- and then to ridicule. Some of it necessary and long overdue but some of it unnecessary, unfair and for all the wrong reasons. Somehow having immature children lying around stoned out of their minds, sexually promiscuous, unwashed, unemployed, unreasonable and uncompromising can't possibly have been the proper forum for appropriate change. Yet change we did, to what some say was the beginning of the end for the United States as a world power. An entire school of thought says that we never recovered from the Viet Nam era spending or attitude. A nightmare of a time which destroyed much of a generation. The "me" generation arrived holding out their hands for entitlements. The Welfare state had arrived. George Orwell (writer of "1984") would be so pleased. During all this time we were still primarily a creditor nation!

The economy started to unravel dramatically as the 1970's came upon us. The Great Society needed blood to feed upon and past and present mistakes took their toll. High government spending and an expansionary monetary policy was finally catching up with us. Government regulations became more and more stringent creating massive paper shuffling at all levels of business. Greed created a wage-price spiral out of control, interest rates rose and productivity declined. The battle between the Monetarists (control economy by the money supply) and the Keynesians (tax and spend, spend, spend!) reached epidemic proportions. The federal deficit was becoming quite large. Finally, along came OPEC. Who knows which, or how many of these, caused the problem? The problem was finally here.

After Kennedy bought the Presidency in 1960, it was not unreasonable to think we might elect a slow thinking movie star to the same office. We were ready for simple folk's answers and Reagan told us what we wanted to hear. Or at least he was smart enough to listen to what his puppet masters told him to say and do. Some of it even worked. Tight money policy brought inflation under control. Sharp reductions in income tax rates were calculated to ignite the consumer spending locomotive and it happened. On the other hand, deregulation brought on a host of problems and made some people rethink their position on the necessity of some regulation in the essential fields like transportation. The Gramm-Rudman-Hollings Act served as further evidence that Congress is a joke, cannot be trusted and Congressional mandates mean nothing. Then there was the great Savings and Loan Debacle which occurred on Reagan's watch, likely due in part to the go-go mentality of the 1980's, when the thirst for profits outweighed common sense. A faint memory whispers to me that Banks & Savings institutions were given a sacred trust when we allowed then the use of our money. Instead, ex-developers with influential friends were given S & L's as toys; to rape and pillage as they pleased while the Junk Bond Kings of Wall Street took whatever was left of Middle America's money.

One of the keys to even attempting an understanding of economics is to acknowledge that it is simply not simple. What one strives for is to know how any one variable is simultaneously affected by all or many of the others. To picture this, imagine a mobile which is manipulated by a pull or release from the Federal Reserve Board. Much of this concept was outlined by Milton Friedman. The pull or release either lowers or raises the money supply. The pull is a raising of the discount rate although it can also be accomplished by changing bank reserve requirements or being a buyer in the open money market. This pull will occur because inflation has set in and the Feds will try to tame it by choking off economic expansion. Inflation benefits those invested in real estate, commodities, gold and collectibles. Prime rates, Treasury Bills, money market funds, Certificates of Deposits and the cost of mortgage money all rise as demand for credit outstrips supply. The saver is happy but the home-buyer faces higher rates and the economy slows. Due to tight credit, businesses stop buying new parts and spending money to expand. Unsold inventories pile up and workers begin to face unemployment. Consumer spending now moderates which further hurts business and exacerbates unemployment. GNP will go down. A trade imbalance or deficit on our part means we buy overseas items with dollars, creating an overabundance of dollars which foreign countries then sell to get back their own currency. Since there are more dollars purchasing goods than other currency buying our goods, the imbalance drives down the dollar's value. Moderating consumer spending should cause imports to go down and the trade deficit narrows. Ideally, the dollar will rise as foreign countries need dollars to buy our exports. This assumes that the exports stay up which, unfortunately, is rarely the case as the very slipping of foreign currencies against the dollar and a slackened demand for their goods causes other countries to enter a slow-down period also. Now we have transferred our gloom overseas as they face the same cycle. Because our income and tax revenues have fallen our federal budget deficit rises. A high federal deficit means the government's demand for money forces even higher interest rates for themselves and everyone else, as well as squeezes out corporate borrowers. Production is now down and unemployment is rising. The stock market falls as corporate earnings nosedive. Just in the nick of time inflation now begins to ease, interest rates turn down and inflationary items also come down. Bond prices therefore will go up. The feds begin to pump money into the system in three ways: with lower rates, buying paper (Treasury Instruments) which puts money into play and lowering reserve requirements. Corporations begin to borrow and increase production. People are hired and unemployment drops. Full production capacity means full employment (good) but causes inflation which must be stopped (bad). And so we begin again. There are some problems related to this scenario however, which need to at least be mentioned here.

Problem 1. Higher prices of foreign goods do not seem to stop the American consumer from buying them.

Problem 2. Slowdowns increase our federal deficit.

Problem 3. Real estate does not come down as inflation and interest rates subside.

Problem 4. The stock market sometimes does not go down as corporate earnings go down, choosing instead to consider good times inflationary and bad times as correcting for a brighter future.

Problem 5. Interest rates sometimes go up to protect a weak dollar which can hardly revive the economy at the same time.

Problem 6. Interest rates go up to stop inflation but also stop the good economic expansion.

Perhaps we expect too much as we become more mature and a little better informed, but for the life of me I can't see how we are still afloat. Is it my imagination or are we simmering beneath the surface? Each year the streets and attitudes in the United States look and sound more like those in Venezuela and Mexico than Germany or Japan. The spread between the wealthy and the poor is increasingly more like that in a third world country. Graft and corruption in government and business must surely be at an all- time high. Huge disparities exist between the salaries of those at the top of major corporations and those in the trenches. Has it always been this way? It doesn't matter. That's why we read Charles Dickens; to learn from the past and our mistakes. The spread between Japan's highest paid personnel and the lowest is "only" a factor of 7 or 8. Ours approaches 120! But at least these businessmen/women appear to be doing something productive. Are we sure that we can't balance the budget by simply capping our talent industries at a reasonable figure (say $300,000 a year) and apply the rest to the deficit. Yeah, it would probably take a long time- like a year or two.

Much has been made of the so called 3 major trading blocks - Europe, North/South America and the

Orient. Each has a source of inexpensive labor and markets for the more sophisticated products of the industrialized partners. Can we make this system work or are we merely creating competition for ourselves with our own money being lent to them? We don't seem to have a time frame as to how long this will take. We also have a problem in that Latin America may be the least reliable and desirable L.D.C (Lesser Developed Country) partner of the three respective trading groups. Latin America is not as well educated as its Eastern Europe or Asian counterpart, has a poorer work ethic, despite Eastern Europe's fifty years under communism, and has weather not conducive to productivity. Mexico is certainly a good example. They have practiced backward policies for four centuries governed by graft, corruption and laziness. Here is a risky ally and business associate. I suppose that we should mention NAFTA & GATT here. They both seem like good ideas which will help level that playing field. Problem is it does take time and people can be hurt as jobs are lost. No one cares that the "net job gain" will be in our favor if their job was lost and they can't get one of the new gained ones. Progress was already being made in opening up economies naturally and those who don't want to be opened to competition will continue to find the many loopholes available.

Free enterprise works only in a vacuum where all sides play on a level playing field. For all of our Colonialist reputation, we don't hold our own against the protectionism thrown at us by both European and the Asian countries. In other words, everyone. No doubt

Japan is the most glaring offender if only because of our close relationship with them.

General consensus has it that the weak dollar is positive because international customers will buy our cheaper goods. I am inclined to agree with the contrarians since the most recent several years of weakness has done little or nothing to help in any way other than maybe benefiting those at the very top in a few exporting firms. The inflow of investment funds into dollars may be in large part due to the dollar being the currency basis for trade and business (called the reserve currency) and if we continue on our current course that may not continue as countries chose the stronger Mark or Yen. There are three main flows affecting the exchange markets- trade, money market and portfolio capital. If trade flows are moving the market, then competitiveness is the most important factor; if money market flows are dominating, the key is interest rate differentials; if portfolio capital predominates, it is the valuation of the bond and equity markets. Over the past few years, portfolio capital has been moving the market, to the confusion of analysts who tend to concentrate on economic factors such as inflation and interest rate differentials (Persaud, 1995).

One of the oldest ways to examine this issue is called purchasing power parity (PPP) which states that a basket of goods in one country should cost about the same as in another. Therefore as inflation rises in one country, its currency will devalue accordingly against a stronger (less inflationary) one. The only weakness in this theory is that not all goods are traded across national boundaries. The trade deficit is a related issue. When there was a gold standard the mechanism automatically brought everyone back into balance. Now currency depreciation does that.

A depreciated dollar is supposed to make our exports more attractive but the problem is it also increases the price of imports. If one believes that consumers will purchase quality at any price, e.g. Japanese cars) we are merely inflating the price we must pay for goods. Additionally, American manufacturers don't really attempt to see if a large price difference will help them. They merely raise their own prices up to just under that of the import. All that has happened is the consumer pays more. The only reason the United States has been able to run a persistent balance of payment deficit and steady dollar devaluation without inflation is that trade is still a relatively small part of our GNP. The wrong attitude and practices are in place, however, so we have nothing of which to be proud. Another way to reduce demand for foreign goods, and therefore eliminate the trade deficit, is to raise interest rates. It also attracts money market flows. The problem is it reduces demand for our own products as well and high interest rates generally always damage an economy even as it hopefully stifles inflation. Portfolio capital seeking better corporate bonds and equity values will leave faster than any money market flows come in. There is also the psychological aspect whereby a country like Germany can get away with low interest rates and still have a very strong currency because investors correctly perceive that the Bundesbank will act ruthlessly to eliminate inflation (because of their experiences before WWII with the Weimar Republic).

Where portfolio capital goes is a question we never get to ask because the United States doesn't have much. Our corporations do, just our government doesn't. Because we are a large debtor nation and the Japanese, for example, are a creditor nation they have the funds to sway the markets. These funds are a function of high savings rates. Japan has the ability to do to our currency what we did to Mexico's because of a lack of confidence. From all this we begin to see a composite picture of a country with weak currency-high inflation, high debts, a high trade deficit and the inability or unwillingness to tackle its problems. Hmmmmm.

The good news for us is the foreign exchange market is not an efficient one because bank dealers, corporate treasurers and central banks all have different views and motives. These markets are also volatile. This is known in academic jargon as heterogeneous auto-regressive conditional heteroskedasticity (Investopedia, 1996). What a great phrase.

As to the demise of the dollar as a reserve currency, like the death of Mark Twain, it appears to be somewhat exaggerated. Certainly at one time it was used 100% as the reserve currency. But we no longer are so overwhelmingly omnipotent. The United States accounts for only 20% of world output and 14% of exports so it's not too unreasonable to expect world currency holdings to more closely approximate their national output. Actually we still are the reserve currency of choice 60% of the time and any demise is perceived as modest and manageable with no sense of crisis.

Riva Batra, an economist at Southern Methodist University, is a doomsday writer along the lines of Paul Erdman (The Crash of '79), Joe Granville, industrialist Harry Figgie and financier Peter Peterson. Mr. Batra wrote a book called The Great Depression of 1990 which advised investors to "sell the farm" in anticipation of the impending crash (Batra, 1987).Even though his timing was premature he still swears we are all in serious trouble. Most of his theory is based on long term economic cycles such as the wave cycle espoused by the Russian economist Nikolai Kondratieff. Mr. Kondratieff's cycle term is 60 years or so. Both of these theories operate on the biblical-like view that if you sin you must pay for it. So in finance, if you persist in being irresponsible, economic disaster will follow. I don't believe the first and I'm not sure about the second.

Yet we continue to be irresponsible and get away with it. Even as the dollar lost 75% of its value against the Japanese Yen and German Mark over the last twenty five years, figures state our living standard kept rising and unemployment remained trivial by comparison to the past. The question is, "was the increase evenly distributed and are the unemployment figures accurate?" Looking back twenty years later, other than Japan's problems, has anything changed? It lends credibility to the expression, "the more things change, the more things stay the same." Many studies contradict any higher living standards. My guess is that there are a number of unaccounted for White Anglo-Saxon Protestant Males over 40 who may not feel it's trivial. The media is too busy feeling sorry for the hungry in Africa, young black gang members, women in business, gays in the military and welfare mothers. Not that these are issues to be ignored but let's not lose sight of other issues. In our quest to right the injustices forced upon the black ghetto children we have overlooked the white underclass found not only in the slums of Detroit, Boston, New York and Baltimore but smaller towns like Portland, Maine, Duluth, Minn. and Waterloo, Iowa. The report also challenges the belief that the college- educated are immune from wage stagnation. Even the real wages of the college- educated group have declined nearly 3%. In England there are able bodied men who have never worked a day in their lives. That sounds great until you live it. Then the sickening lack of hope, depression and total disregard for life makes the drudgery of every day not fit for upright man. It's time we learned from those who have gone before us. We should be concerned because it may be our plight as well. It is also time to do something for those individuals. That something is to provide education and meaningful employment for them. To be sure, technology is how we have improved our production over the last 20-30 years, not any increased labor effort. To be sure also, there will be individuals who cannot be trained on the new technology. That does not mean they are to be cast aside or thrown away. I cannot believe that is the direction society is headed, but to date we have not utilized the spare time created by technology in ways to benefit all of us. It appears that technology has made some of us work that much harder while others have been put out of work. Education alone will not solve our problems either. To be fair, we should also mention those under-employed in the Barrios of Mexico, Venezuela and the newly freed of Eastern Europe. There are lessons here as well, for we can observe the new class of brash capitalists with their cellular telephones, sleek Mercedes and disregard for their fellow man. Greed and corruption is more naked there but I doubt there's much difference in the corporate boardrooms of America. Let's face it, take away the sugar coating and the basic premise of Capitalism is principled in greed and avarice. Competition means destroying your enemy. Capitalism takes time to implement and then more time to weed out the carpetbaggers. Communism at least gave people security. It still appears that a little of both would be in order if we are to give incentive yet care for those unable to cope. To observe examples of this, one needs only to go east to China and South Korea. China makes no excuses for its measured and scrutinized modernization under semi-capitalistic guidelines. South Korea though, has fooled the world for thirty years, throughout their economic miracle of growing 1,500% and having per capita income grow eight-fold since 1960. Most westerners are unaware that during that time banks were nationalized, detailed 5 year plans were promulgated, and legal systems were lubricated by coerced bribes, extralegal payments and reciprocal favors. Theirs has not been an egalitarian society. In many ways its high leverage, cheap government credits, micro-managing technocrats, office corps ministries and incestuous

governmental/corporation/trading company relationship was a poor man's version of the Japanese model. And it worked wonders. Only now is Japan going through a restructuring. But even if some changes have to be made, they both have had a long prosperous upswing during a time when the United States and its system have experienced a rough road. In a recent article in the Washington Post we learn that, once again, the Japanese, facing almost the same problems economically as the United States, have come up with a humanitarian solution. Instead of dumping fired middle managers on the street they "farm them out" to wherever they are needed and make up any wage difference. There is also no longer guaranteed advancement in position or income. But the gentle means of incorporating this strategy is to give an upcoming manager ten years to prove herself/himself, after which, if they don't succeed they will be relegated to another path with a slight reduction in pay. Although I like this methodology I admit it has not had time to be proven viable.

It's bothersome that those who indicate we are not going to come crashing down in flames seem to say only that we will continue to be consumed in a slow moving cancerous way. That begs the question, "would you rather be eaten by the tiger in one gulp or in several leisurely bits?" In other words, it looks like a lot of downside exposure and very little upside possibilities. We are barely out of the last recession (many are still in it) and the brakes are being applied. For all of the Fed's tweaking and fine-tuning of the economy we still do not seem to know what it takes to have sustained growth without accelerating inflation.

Can a country that constantly runs a trade deficit and a budget deficit continue to be the land of opportunity?

Is consumer spending really the way to run an economy? That sounds like Keynesian economics or Roosevelt's New Deal. Can we ever break the political strangle hold which does not allow us to simply half the Defense budget, give welfare only to the old, the children and the truly needy, make able bodied recipients work for their check and keep our nose out of places that don't need us, don't want us and in which we have no business.

For better or worse we likewise don't have a cohesive partnership between our government and corporate America as do the Japanese.

We seem to be perfectly represented currently in the White House by a man who exemplifies all those vacillating qualities that tie us in knots and make us look confused to our allies and enemies alike. Can this be fertile ground for economic progress?

Lately all we do in America is shuffle money. Investment bankers don't put money into exploring for raw materials or building manufacturing facilities; they simply buy and sell companies. And those not involved in that are selling real estate, cars and insurance to each other. What some of them need is to be put back to work on the assembly line doing something productive.

School is still out as to whether we can be a service oriented economy and not be involved in manufacturing. We'll see when the next ground war occurs between us and a worthy opponent.

With the exception of technology we are drifting more toward an economy like Venezuela's and less toward Japan's. Venezuela is still surviving but at a less desirable standard of living. Venezuela is also a good example that a country rich in natural resources will not necessarily do well.

What can be done to correct our myriad of problems and combat the Phoenix rising in the Orient and its cheap labor? We have seen that there are many economic factors which affect the performance of a nation, industry or company. Among those mentioned have been deficit spending, exchange rates and inflation. Also important are interest rates, GNP, unions and price wars. Having laid out the problems we have, it would be less than thorough if we didn't try to address some of these with suggestions as to how to solve them.

As long as we believe there's a possibility of a conventional ground war we should be reinforcing our basic manufacturing capabilities; Steel, Farming, Textiles, Rubber, Plastics and Energy. However, if someone does it cheaper, find a way to use them on a piece meal basis, still maintain control of critical technology and spend the profit spread on training. Our management strategy of outsourcing cautions us to always maintain management control of the outsourced portion. This is a necessary condition for a strong and dynamic economic base anyway, industrial capacity along with a skilled work force. To this end the government must encourage long term investment in industry, support small businesses and encourage private finance to become involved. It also needs a tax system which encourages investment rather than evasion.

If we must continue a deficit for some period, we should at least fund it by pushing for direct investment in our factories and businesses like South-East Asia rather than through liquid equity markets which can be withdrawn on a whim and make us vulnerable.

No foreign aid or subsidies (at least while we are unable to balance our budget). PROBLEM: Government lends money to Country A, who buys U.S. Business exports. Ergo that one U.S. Business gets rich. Country A can't produce well enough to pay their debts but they can produce well enough to undercut our other businesses. We pay more in taxes for the bad debt and the money isn't available for other things.

We also don't seem to get paid back when we advance funds to our supposed allies. That holds true whether it's Israel during the last twenty years, France after WWII, or Latin America over and over again.

Let's reduce our Defense budget by cutting waste and actual spending. Or charge for it. There is something anachronistic about being a mercenary. I don't like it but if we insist on doing it, it's better to get paid for it than to do it for free. No reason not to be paid back from Iraqi oil. Instead of reductions over ten years in order to balance the budget we need to see reductions of $150 Billion in defense immediately! Retrain while continuing to pay workers and place them back in service with useful skills. Get out of Germany and France.

Stay out of Civil Wars-but restrict nuclear arms in hostile countries.

I've heard it said that if all the money were divided equally it would all be back in the same hands in a short period of time. So what? If it's that easy, it wouldn't hurt to do it every once in a while-like the lottery. I've heard it said that we should give athletes 3 square meals and a bed-just like a gladiator-that's all they deserve for playing a game. It's just a game!!!! Poor babies. Spare me their whining.

If you want to get on track regarding improving society we need to stop rewarding artistic temperament (meaning bad manners).

Eliminate the real estate, insurance and car dealers profession altogether.

Restrict pay for sports, movie stars, singers etc. Keep it less than teacher's pay and 5-10 times the average pay of the worker. Do this by placing a huge surtax or cap on them. The same goes for Stock profit also per year. Create severe penalties for violations.

Restrict the pay ratio of top businessmen to 10 times that of the lowest paid employee

Minimum wage in 2003 should be $15/hour, not $5. Raise it

No tax under $40k

Why is it we have money to blow on a war but not on education?

Make stock options longer and you have to pay it back if it goes back down

Limit law suit judgment amounts.

Make the unemployed work on public projects.

Adapt a clear and enforceable "Level Field" policy on trade. Exempt those items that relate to national security and infant industries.

Strengthen the dollar! -If we produce a desired product in a quality fashion it will be exported and bought at any price within reason. Incoming goods will be cheaper and help to raise our standard of living. Individual exporters may cut deals if they wish. That way they are only reducing their own profits.

Establish a national health policy with free medicine for all and control the costs.

Eliminate governments unnecessary jobs (retrain & put them to work doing something productive).

Keep the government out of things that don't concern then such as abortion, segregation, gays in the military etc...

Get serious about elimination of government waste and poor purchasing habits.

Force the government to learn to cooperate and assist industry.

As dull and trite as it may seem, education must be given it's proper priority- in the work force, to those who are unemployed or underemployed and to the children.

Train staff working overseas in local cultures, languages and courtesy for a better reputation and better lines of communication.

Concentrate on the little projects (Peace Corp types) that help the average person in the lesser developing countries.

INFLATION WILL BE BACK! Inflation is one of the most onerous forms of theft. It affects those who save, normally the elderly, and happens in such a manner you don't even realize what's happening. Continue to address this in every way possible.

In summary, there is certainly a need for change. Economic policy should follow Aristotle's Golden Mean- "moderation in all things". Let's lead with a strong dose of capitalism but eliminate its ugly side as much as possible, meanwhile pulling only the positive points from socialism and even communism.

If there is no orderly world economic market there is no market for banks and their lending capabilities. As David Stockman and Arthur Laffer (Supply side thinkers under President Reagan) would no doubt concur, there can be no "trickle down" without a place from which to trickle. Certainly the banking industry has been on the cutting edge since its inception. Since the moneylenders in the temples of Egypt those who were involved in banking were generally the beneficiaries of positive growth and huge profits. Like the United States however, the industry is maturing and competition is increasing dramatically both from within the U.S. and overseas. In the past there have been growth industries such as farming, electric power & light, appliances, chemicals, aluminum, foundries, textiles manufacturing and railroads. Who could have forecast that the boom industries of the past could be the Dinosaurs of today?

That insert from 1996 may be a bit premature looking back from 2015 to 1996, spot on in many ways yet not so much in others.

One theory of what caused the 2008 financial crisis was, like the roaring 20s, there had been a previous period of gorging. A light went on in the mind of some little mouse deep in the belly of some big bank and they began to see the risk. In the stampede toward the door the light became brighter and shown on all the folly. "Once more unto the breach." See? History is there as a learning tool if we observe. In 2014 the Feds, by keeping interest rates low, are actually forcing conservative savers out on the risk curve to get a decent yield.

Sometimes we can look to the near past for answers and tell what will happen to us by observing the decline that's further along in other countries. Study them to see what leaders do, level of debauchery, level of currency debasement., level of taxes, look for price controls, more government regulations, takeover of private-sector factories, and governing by decree. All these developments are standard playbook steps as a nation enters the final stage of governmental deterioration. Most of these have taken place in the EU and the US and are being expanded upon.

Price Fixing in Venezuela has caused artificially low prices on many goods. So people buy up all the supplies and hoard them, which do not get replaced because producers hoard. Historically, food shortages tend to occur in the latter stages of a decline, just prior to collapse of the system. (In the last year, food prices have nearly doubled in Venezuela.) Funny thing about a food shortage, it's dangerous to not have it, but if others find out you have it, it's dangerous to have it because someone will want to take it. A food crisis is a major cause and effect of hyperinflation.

Why is it that most politicians and economists don't see the vicious circle that occurs when you print money? First, a natural deflationary process begins, usually to wring out the excess from an inflationary bubble. Thinking this is somehow a bad thing, the Central bankers, with the blessing of the politicians and economists, begin to print money to combat that deflation. Inflation increase prices, wages can't keep up, people need to liquidate assets to pay for essentials, more assets hit the market and the assets deflate, so they print more money to combat deflation in the prices of assets. If the government doesn't get its act together in time and stop printing, the result will probably be hyperinflation.

History also tells us that when a governments is in bad shape, like the United States, they have almost always looked for ways to squeeze their citizens for every penny they can get away with.

It isn't as though good advisers don't warn the powers that be. Back to that history lesson.

CHAPTER THREE - INFLATION

Bubbles

"New bubbles make us forget the previous bubble"

Inflation and its advocates have been covered at length in another book so this is just a condensed summary of the pros and cons.

Inflation in the purest sense is the increase in the overall cost of living due to the government printing un-backed money, It is not caused by pressure for wage increases, or by rising oil prices, or by consumer demand, although they may contribute somewhat. An inelastic product may be the exception to this. The increase in production in China isn't any more deflationary than the increase in oil prices is inflationary. Yes prices did go up due to higher oil prices (greedy everybody), poor alternative energy policy, high food prices caused by stupid ethanol production and subsidies [politicians], greedy Wall Street speculators and some really foolish import/export policies); we were just unwilling to reduce our standard of living accordingly. So instead of our standards going down we printed money or refinanced our houses. The argument suggests that wars typically cause inflation but might create productivity.

Politicians don't like recessions. Forgetting for a moment that recessions usually are necessary to squeeze out the inflation because of an unjustified previous expansion, they are necessary and do serve the purpose of getting people back to reality. Expansive monetary policy (Inflation) is supposed to create boom times, more trade, factories producing at full tilt, production and resources are being bought; but costs begin to go up, wages go up- all of which lead to rising prices and that cools off the economy, demand falls and unemployment rises while prices remain high. Cycle complete.

One of the problems governments have is it is a lot harder to drain money from the economy than put it in. People are more than willing to ride an inflation wave upwards as they see all their assets and hopefully wages, increase. They then immediately forget that and do not want to go back to where they were. That's especially true in real estate. Everyone wants to take personal credit for the increase in price, like they actually did anything to cause it. That is also true for say, oil cost increases that should go back down as the price of oil does, or the CEO pay that got out of hand for whatever reason you feel fits your imagination. Another foible in the system is that money pumped into the system goes to the financial section because it has a tough time going to the real world. It could be that main street does actually wise up every once in a while. There is a bit of inconsistency here regarding the attitudes of the average person. History has shown that the mal distribution of money to the financial section and to pay of their leaders generally is not good for an economy.

Deflation

Deflation is just the opposite, a reduction of money in circulation which results in a decrease in the general price level. Our friends in Washington say deflation causes lower wages and/or unemployment. Well, let's see: The cost of living comes down, houses become more affordable, interest rates come down making loans cheaper, food, energy, and education all become less expensive. Or should. Educational health care and energy have not decreased their prices. What is the problem? Hello conspiracy theory.

Warren Buffett has said that deflation is worse than inflation. Maybe for him because he has a lot of assets that go up (or down). Not so much for those of us who have few assets and with the same wages need to buy things that have gone up in price. The deflation is bad crowd continues by saying, when prices go down, people wait to buy, because prices might be cheaper later. That small part of the equation may be true, but there are other factors- so figure a way as a government to stop this.

How did the government solve the problem? By printing money and going to war. We gave 18-year-old kids guns and sent them off to kill other 18-year-olds.

Now if I had the solution to this mess I would be worth much more than minimum wage, but here goes. Deflation usually occurs as a result of having to purge an inflationary period. So stop inflating.

Sometimes I feel like I am Winston in 1984, listening to Big Brother simply delete the truth and swear to something else. To hear some of these pundits talk, the dollar really hasn't decreased 97% in value since 1913. Kind of like an Arab, or any anti-Israeli, denying the Holocaust.

The "deflation is bad" camp continues with the following skewed logic or outright lies: Computers are cheaper. That old Hedonics argument. Housing prices haven't gone up in 10 years (By whose standards? Higher education isn't worth as much as it used to be (too much student loan debt and not enough jobs). That last one has to do with the inflation of the cost of education, not the value of an education, plus poor planning by the government to get jobs for people. I think we can pretty much nail the lid on the coffin when your society believe there is little value in education. Besides, doesn't the high cost of education corroborate the inflation side of the argument? Electricity is cheaper- seriously? At 11-20 cents per KWH I wonder if my wages have gone up correspondingly. Remember, adjustment for inflation assumes you are participating in the inflation game. Books are cheaper (who knows or cares- most people don't read anyway). Movies are cheaper. Where do they get such false information? Music is basically free if watched on YouTube. True but a minor part of your life and the economy. Or at least it should be.

If we are being told deflation is the norm and our government is preventing it by causing the inflation, what does that say about the motives of your government?

Forget about a 10 year time span. Think about 100-200 years. And the wage gap. Is your life better? Can you buy more or less with your money?

According to the Backing Theory, an increase in the money supply, accompanied by an equal increase in assets, will have no effect on prices. Backing means there is gold (or some specie) somewhere stored in the same -or some- amount (but you can't have it!). Convertibility means you can actually have it.

Also, thinking that the price of any given good is likely to increase over time, consumers believe it's better to make purchases sooner than later, which also helps the economy. But high inflation tends to reduce long-term capital formation since there is no incentive to save.

Further in considering what consumers might believe; Psychology is a powerful motivator. Sometimes people do irrational things because they believe it to be in their best interest. In economics that's called Animal Spirits, when attitudes either optimistic or pessimistic can lead to self-fulfilling recessions or economic booms even if the fundamentals say otherwise. Peoples' emotions often will trump whatever plan or theory is being sought. Concern about future incomes leads to a fall in consumption that leads to less sales by companies that caused the recession that was being feared in the first place. Same thing happens with companies that cut back on plant and equipment purchases because they fear a recession. Without new plant and equipment there will be less output. Sure enough a recession will come. Think "Chicken or the Egg.

When the government isn't printing money out of thin air, it's borrowing money from taxpayers, giving it to Wall Street and the commercial banks so they can lend it back to the taxpayers at a profit. Whoever came up with that as a way to do business?

Come to think of it, I guess Hank Paulson was the best man for the Treasury job, after all, his firm created the toxic investments causing all the trouble. Even if you could get him to admit that Goldman did anything wrong he would blame it on some underling. Gosh, how could you expect a CEO to know anything, right? He was busy making speeches and getting bonuses. No responsibility there. Ditto with Tim Geitner. What a job. Encourage taxpayers to spend, take their money, create worthless paper money and give the goodies to their old buddies on Wall Street.

Did you ever wonder why government economists favor inflation over deflation? Hint. Everybody always wants to get something for nothing. Inflation is the best way to get rich quick. Deflation would therefore hurt the shysters more. Inflation is based on monopoly and control. Deflation levels the playing field a little at least, or narrows the wealth gap some. There are a lot of rich people who rely on that inflation to continue their monopoly

The only reason for inflation is to steal from savers without their knowing it to pay off government debts with cheaper money.

Another negative is savers and investors are forced to take on risk, in order to get a decent return.

Wages rise nominally so it looks like we are doing better. Money illusion is when we think we are getting richer when they get a raise.

Inflation only helps those who are massively indebted, inefficient and getting the free handouts- the governments, banks, big corporations and the rich. Inflation raises people up into a higher tax bracket, giving money to the government. If you are still worried about the effect of deflation on debt still being owed at the old rates and money values, not a problem. Simply readjust them downward along with the deflation levels. Paying down debt (or high savings) places the paid off debt in a bank where in theory it gets lent out again so there should be no change. Unless savers are just putting under a mattress.

Inflation skews wealth distribution since things like the stock market and real estate are mostly owned by rich people. Inflation will reverse-redistribute income from those on fixed incomes, such as pensioners, and shift it to the speculators and the rich. It also redistributes wealth from those who lend to those who borrow. Finally, the poor and middle class get hurt more when there is inflation because they spend a bigger percentage of their money on basics. It costs the rich the same to eat, drive, insure, etc. and they have all that left over money as discretionary.

The true increase and effects of inflation have been veiled by what the government calls Hedonics, which says that the product has been improved and that's why it's more expensive- so the price gets reduced back down and it is not inflation. Your government does this to keep adjustments low on things they owe, like Social Security.

The difference between government and investor money is investor money is taken out of circulation from somewhere else while simply printing came from nowhere and only adds money to the system. This is true also on a private scale. The sale of real estate or stocks or art or cars, at an inflated price, will have to be paid for by a buyer at the inflated price. So, the increased liquidity of the seller is offset by a diminished liquidity of the buyer.

Why no inflation (in some things)? There is no velocity because the banks are hoarding the money and not lending it. The money the Fed is printing through QE is mostly going into financial speculation, not into expanding the money supply through lending and spending. The banks are at odds with the Fed policy and not honoring the verbal understanding. The Feds want to prevent deflation (whether you agree with the policy or not) while the banks are causing deflation by not lending. Perhaps a little because China (Vietnam and India), due to low wages and other costs, is producing cheap products for us and themselves. Another possibility is what's called the "Output Gap." There is room in manufacturing to produce without prices rising.

Unbacked Money printing occurs like so: The Fed buys bonds directly issued by the government, which the government then spends. The government is supposed to pay back the Fed for the money they got. Or, rather than having the Treasury issue bonds and sell them to the Fed to get money, the Fed (who simply printed it), just gave the Treasury the money for free. Then the government would buy bonds, from banks supposedly, who would then later have to pay the bonds off/buy them back from the Treasury. Then the Treasury would pay back that money to the Fed and we would be even. So the government first either sells bonds to the Fed to get money and then gives it to banks (or buys bank bonds-same thing), which is intended to cause inflation.

You raise interest rates to curb inflation (a weak dollar) by restoring confidence and strengthening the dollar. High rates attracts investment and strengthens the currency.

Stocks and other asset prices rise, people borrow cheaply and spend more, which should promote growth. Yet, empirical evidence suggests that money creation leads directly to devaluation of the dollar, meaning people have less money to spend and products become less affordable. With falling incomes and therefore falling demand for products, the desired demand for factories, equipment and housing will fall. This recreates the problem of excessive saving and encourages the recession to continue. It would be Classical, free market thinking to allow the recession. Raising interest rates causes foreign capital to flow in. They must also buy dollars to buy the bonds. Both cause the currency to increase. The bad news is it crowds out corporate borrowing. The currency appreciates so goods cost more so foreigners buy less (decreases net exports). But imports cost less and we import more than we export so that's a good thing and should stop inflation and help savors. Inflation believers say lower interest rates and a lower dollar should mean our products are cheaper to buy for other countries. But, don't we import more than we export? If so, doesn't that mean all those Gucci bags, perfume and BMWs are more expensive? Would you rather your currency buy more or less? Price fluctuation doesn't seem to stop us from buying regardless.

It seems the one thing both political parties can agree upon is "we got to spend money."

When Central banks buy bonds, they don't use existing assets; they simply create money out of thin air and give it to the seller of the bonds. In return, the banks receive in assets like government bonds or mortgage backed securities. I suspect the mortgage backed securities are not even counted when calculating our debt burden and debt to GDP ratios.

Later Central banks can either sell the securities in the public market, or hold them to maturity. Of course, the second never happens- it always gets rolled over. This cash came from selling securities that were originally purchased with newly printed money. Therefore, it should have been destroyed. But it never is. Central banks are never going to sell their bonds back into the market. They know they can never unload so many bonds without causing a crash in the debt market. What's worse, it is given to the government, for what reason I will never know.

When the central bank prints dollars out of thin air, they are stealing from everyone who currently holds dollars because they are diluting the supply, more of something makes each item less valuable. The created money always goes to investors, speculators and art buyers. The rich get richer. Remember the trickle-down theory from Arthur Laffer and Reagan? I guess that means there will be a bunch of new factories and plenty of new jobs, right

The Twentieth Century

It has been a busy one for innovation and new inventions. Along with all the good came the ugliness of inflation.

It is hard to believe that we are the best apple in a bad barrel. We merely increased prices 23-fold in the Twentieth century with most other countries being worse. Notice the difference between 14 and 23? Someone is getting rich or else someone's research is wrong.

Exchange rates don't mean anything unless they adjust in concert with the inflation. If that be so, you are merely breaking even. If the price of food increases as the exchange rate, everything stays the same. And vice versa. If the exchange rate increases and food increases, you haven't gained anything.

Why did these countries succeed in controlling inflation during the Twentieth century when other countries failed? It appears that: they had small, open economies dependent on trade, they all had independent monetary authorities or currency boards (this ties the currency to that of a country with good anti-inflationary policies) that avoided an over-issue of currency (minimize control over monetary policy), none of them suffered periods of economic or political chaos that might have led to high rates of inflation (even though both the Netherlands and Singapore were occupied during World War II) , and none of the governments have used large government deficits to fund social and defense programs that could have produced inflation.

Is there a tendency for certain geographical/ ethnic areas to inflate? In general the Asian countries seem less prone with some exceptions. Did Indonesia suffer inflation because of the Spanish culture? Many South American countries don't seem to have the hang of avoiding it. The European countries mainly went through a period of hyperinflation after a War, and with the collapse of the Soviet Union. The African colonies did fine with Currency Boards tied to European currencies until the 1960s when they became independent.

Every one of the countries listed here was unable and/or unwilling to pay for government expenditures through raising taxes, choosing to print money instead. Over time, this action becomes self-defeating as the inflation reduces real government receipts making the deficit even larger until the economy collapsed into hyperinflation.

Prices in most countries had doubled, tripled or quadrupled during World War I, but after the war deflation set in. The United Kingdom and other countries tried to return to the Gold Standard, reestablishing the exchange rates that had existed prior to World War I.

China's inflationary collapse had more to do with the civil war that followed World War II than with the war itself. The Communist parts of China had much lower inflation rates during the Civil War than the Nationalist parts of China. Greece suffers inflation the way some of us suffer a cold, and just about as often. It would be tough to not realize there are some nationalistic traits and most of theirs centers around not wanting to do much work.

Poor economic policies create hyperinflation, it's a political choice. Countries suffer inflation because they are unwilling to deal with the economic problems.

When the Soviet Union collapsed in 1989 many of the countries that made up the former Soviet Union suffered hyperinflation.

The source of inflation is the unwillingness of governments to balance their books and avoid deficits.

Price inflation imposes many costs. Unexpected inflation redistributes money from creditors to debtors and from employees to employers. It can wipe out the value of fixed assets. Asset inflation such as that in the stock market and real estate creates artificial wealth, encouraging firms and consumers to borrow beyond their means. When the asset inflation ends, firms and individuals are unable to pay their debts leading to declines in demand and to economic slowdowns. The problem is asset inflation is deceptive. You think you are richer than you are.

Inflation occurs because governments are unwilling to deal with the economic problems they face. Germany and Austria, perhaps having learned their lesson after the First World War, avoided inflation after World War II. In fact, Germany has proven that one can learn from one's mistakes and still practices a better economic policy than most as of 2015. Czechoslovakia avoided the high inflation throughout the Twentieth century while their neighbors did not. Some Central American countries did have inflation and some did not. Inflation is not something you can't control. In the 1800s after the inflation of the Napoleonic Wars, the United States, United Kingdom, France and other countries made sure that paper money inflation did not return for a century. The United States even reacted better during the second oil crisis than they did in the first one.

History has also shown that it only gets worse, the longer you allow it to fester and it is never any good for economic investment.

The countries with the best records on inflation in the Twentieth century were the countries that had independent Central Banks. The Central Bank must have a commitment to fighting inflation at all costs.

Most agree that fighting inflation is the primary goal of a Central Bank. So how come ours is doing just the opposite? .

After World War II and on through 1989 a global market didn't exist, plus the excessive indebtedness of the 1920-1930s had been eliminated (the Private/public debt ratio dropped from around 295% to 139% and savings rose to 28% (Hoisington & Hunt, 2014). Low indebtedness/high savings. Shortly after World War II ended the Russians and Chinese removed a huge portion of the world's population from global trade, reducing economies of scale and increasing inflation. With sustainable debt levels the US entered the post-war boom and prosperity.

Low inflation and insufficient demand are both symptoms of extreme over-indebtedness. So how can increasing indebtedness raise inflation? That is the game plan, isn't it?

Facing weak domestic demand, foreign producers cut prices on goods coming here, and this forced domestic producers to match those lower prices. More to the point, the domestic producers never miss a chance to raise prices to match imports when they should be keeping prices lower to build market share.

If inflation is such a good deal why not everyone just do it and be done with it? Someone has to be losing somewhere or why bother? Wages must keep up with the price increases for the workers to stay even. But it's relatively easy with some research to see that certain things do not keep up. The minimum wage argument, whether a good or bad thing, clearly shows that it is not equivalent to what it was in years past. Even acknowledging the government's intent to pay off debt cheaper, doesn't the other side suffer somehow?

Even if wages keep up with prices, what about people who no longer earn wages, or rely on a fixed income?

Debt

If debt is a problem, it has been managed for so long that it no longer seems like a problem. It has no meaning to the average person. Big mistake. All we're talking about here is when, not if, a serious problem will explode.

How can you have debt grow 2.68 times GDP and not have a debt crisis? Even that's probably not a fair assessment because GDP is made up of inflation numbers also. The better way to look at it is that debt grew over 800% from 1983 to 2009. The good thing to remember (I guess) is that China debt grew from $1 trillion to $27.35 trillion or 2,635% while GDP grew from $1 trillion to $9 trillion (Amadeo, 2015) (Dent, China's Economic Spiral, 2015). Just remember, two wrongs do not make a right.

Millions of people including financial commentators, Dick Chaney, and many economists believe that debt doesn't matter. Live in the moment. But since Americans don't save any more that means you are living on someone else's dime.

In 1964 US federal debt was 14.8% of tax revenues. In 1989 it took 43% of tax revenues and in 1993 it was 52% of taxes. In 2013 it went back down to 15% thanks to the artificially low interest rates. Look out when that changes.

Three things can happen. The government can extract tax revenues from you, inflate the currency to keep the ball rolling, or go bankrupt.

Debt is actually hindering the recovery

An assumption is that the massive creation of new currency units by the Fed will eventually cause significant price inflation.

Others argue that the Fed does control the money supply because they pay relatively higher interest on the reserves/currency units that banks keep on deposit with them which tempts the banks to leave the money there and not lend it.

Economic Hardship

In the 20th century, inflation has been identified as being a major source of concern and economic hardship for the poor, far more so than for the rich (Fischer & Modigliani, 1978). During previous long-run inflationary periods, real wages have stagnated (Desilver, 2014). When general prices rise, wages tend to rise more slowly (if at all).

Chronic inflation is associated with economic hardship, perceptions (as a bare minimum) of societal injustice and declining well-being, political dissatisfaction and general malaise (Dudwa, 2015). Political-scientific studies suggest that public opinion sours on incumbent governments when inflation worsens (Lewis-Beck & Stegmaier, 2007)

The difficulty with welfare programs, is that they are costly and increasingly difficult for states to finance when inflation is chronic and their own budgets are strained. Governments are often reluctant to fully index welfare or pensions to prices (Fischer & Modigliani, 1978), making the real value of these payments lower

Job growth is stagnant and even those people who do have a job are not in a position to spend because their incomes are not growing." That goes a long way to explain why consumption growth has been so weak.

On the poor end of the job spectrum the bulk of spending goes to pay for non-durable items, such as gas, food and clothing -- all of which always seem to only go up, never down. If there is any money left that what gets spent on cars, appliances and furniture.

Our creditors, primarily Japan, China and countries of the Middle East, are holding so much of our debt, they really can't afford to let us fail too hard, or too fast. But it can't go on indefinitely and they have long since lost their appetite for US debt.

Causes

What causes inflation and is it better than deflation? Harry Dent also says that if most of the money created went into loans by banks then inflation would be a real threat, but that's not what happened. Gold is an inflation hedge primarily and a crisis hedge secondarily. This isn't an inflationary era despite unprecedented money printing since late 2008 due to demographic decline, debt deleveraging and excess capacity created from the bubble era. Dent says, "Historically, debt and financial asset bubbles always lead to deflation when they burst, not inflation." True, but the deflation happens after the inflation bubble has occurred, so Dent failed to fill in the time line properly. He goes on to say, "Unprecedented money printing has been required to simply offset deflation and hold off another great depression." It is really just the other way around.

Dent says today, gold isn't representative of the information-based economy and it's too costly to be a medium of exchange. What we need is a standard for money creation that limits it more in line with the economic growth."

Dent Research's Rodney Johnson agrees that money printing isn't working. He says in economic theory this might make sense, but in everyday reality, not so much. In theory, a central bank creates money out of thin air and buys bonds from investors, banks, pension funds, etc., which gives those entities more money to buy more bonds which drives down interest rates. Some of the money paid out for the bonds will end up as deposits at banks instead of being reinvested which will give the banks more money to lend. The lower interest rates will be too tempting and consumers and businesses will borrow to buy more stuff. Great theory- not so much reality. Someone forgot to read the instructions to the banks.

The shysters say the trade deficit is not a problem. It's OK for one nation to buys things that it cannot afford and doesn't need with money it doesn't have. Another sells on credit to people who already cannot pay and builds more factories to increase output. What a model. The government urges citizens to buy houses, buy SUVs, and spend, spend, spend-usually on imported foreign goods.

Ask yourself if you were one of these other countries, would you like it if the United States was living beyond its means at your expense?

The argument goes that deflation creates a disincentive for consumers and businesses to spend money. Economic activity slows, unemployment rises and demand declines some more. That fails to consider that consumers don't save forever so ultimately the money gets spent. Yes, falling prices create incentives and the ability to save, that just means a future of economic growth. As to the debt, it's been addressed often. You borrowed it so suffer the consequences. If the government wants to help they can figure a way to reduce that debt somehow but that's a tough assignment because you have the issue of determining who deserves to get help and who is just a speculator who needs to go broke. That's the risk you took when you borrowed in hopes of making a killing. Were you going to share some of that speculative wealth with the rest of us?

There is a worry supposedly, in emerging economies that falling currencies might aggravate inflation. Then how come we don't worry about that when we force our currency down? Isn't that just the opposite of what we are doing and are being asked to believe?

Higher rates bring foreign capital investment so why would we want to lower rates? To be more competitive in exporting when we export less than we import.

It is obvious to anyone who bothers to think about it that an economy that spends more than it earns is in decline and it can't go on indefinitely. At some point other countries will not support this- the removal from dollar denomination by the likes of China and Russia is a first step. At the same time countries are unloading dollars as quickly as they can.

Adam Smith wrote in 1776 that we cannot trust the undertakers of business to look out for anyone but themselves, and so we must handcuff them. His solution was more and better competition. Smith also said: "Our merchants and master manufacturers complain much of the bad effects of high wages in raising the price, and thereby lessening the sale of their goods, both at home and abroad. They say nothing concerning the bad effects of high profits; they are silent with regard to the pernicious effects of their own gains; they complain only of those of other people." How come this is always left out when extolling Smith's backing of a free market society?

I can understand OPEC cramming it down our throats, I just can't understand us taking it. The OPEC oil cartel back in the 1970s really did a number on us. Because we were too stupid, too weak or had ulterior motives, we got our butts handed to us. And we did nothing to obtain alternative energy over the next forty years either. But according to one school, redistribution isn't inflation, just price increases for some. Had we been satisfied to accept a lower standard of living due to higher prices there would have been no inflation (by some definition).

But lots of things have that same effect. When the US government implemented Desegregation back in the 50s and 60s that interfered with market forces. It essentially eliminated competition. Same goes for movements that created safer workplaces. These were not bad. So how to apply these principles to oil. Paying African Americans more and reducing the chances of on-the-job injuries caused inflation (because they raised costs) and redistributed income. Was this justifiable or not? All that is being said here is, be fair and apply the same rules. Maybe even figure out which rules are fair.

So, inflation is a lot of things. Certainly increasing the money supply, especially by simply printing it. That supposedly creates demand. But the outrageous increase in oil prices did the job also. Supply disruption, asset market bubbles. Tough discussion.

Picture if you will; at the mall everything says 50% off. At the car dealers the sticker says 40% off. How about the price of the kid's college education is suddenly 25% of what it was? As a businessman, the price of your raw materials just goes down allowing you to make more profit, pay workers better, establish an investment program, market more, and pay dividends. Any of that bad for you in any way? When you think about it, really, how in the world do they get away with conning you into believing cheaper is ever anything but good? That's, my friend, is deflation. It's intuitive that bargains are a good thing. Common sense even.

Keynesians, Monetarists, and Classicalists

KEYNESIANS believe you should spend money you raised through taxes and borrowing by issuing bonds bought by legitimate sources, not the Fed (Fiscal), but not just printing. Demand drives an economy. Better inflation then unemployment and a business downturn. **MONETARISTS** believe you should print (supply) money and lower interest rates. They also believe business cycles, and unemployment are caused by inadequate demand. Sticky prices lets you increase output in the short run without price increases **CLASSICISTS** believe hands off, stimulation crowds out private investment, lower taxes for a trickle-down effect. Savings translates to investment.

Stagflation throws a wrench into the Keynesian and Monetarist theories. Although it has happened other times, the 1970s were a good recent example of what can go wrong. Both inflation and unemployment were high. Friedman believed the oil crisis in the 1970s caused unemployment but not inflation, mostly because there had already been rising inflation and rising unemployment before that. Why continue with the same plan if that's the case?

CHAPTER FOUR - INEQUALITY

Two Worlds Here in America

What kind of a government panders to the rich while people are homeless and even the middle class is struggling
Many of these people were let go during a downturn caused by the rich and the government.

Our government doesn't punish the rich anymore. On Wall Street you don't go to jail, you get bailed out or settle out of court for a small fine because you're too big to fail.

The government has allowed an entire industry (Finance) to morph into something that adds very little to the world's wealth. Most financial activity is merely shuffling money from one person to another - giving the financial industry an opportunity to collect a commission.

Which came first, the chicken or the egg? Do we not bother to turn down the reality show because it's no use contesting the governmental outcome (inflation, unfair advantages of the rich, and a really lousy government that is so self-serving it can't get anything done or is just bought by the rich; or has the government become what it is because we do nothing except watch reality TV?

This transfer of wealth was created by the Federal Reserve, with the backing, cooperation and input of the White House, Congress, and the biggest banks in the country. Although the claim is that they are doing all this inflating to help out the middle class during the downturn (caused by them by the way), what really happened was the rich got richer because they had access to cheap money to pay off their mortgages, plus because of the availability of cheap money they were able to buy more property.

The rich and powerful point to the stock market as proof that all the silly ideas are working. Besides the fact that only the rich own stocks, take a look at some other examples of what happens with a rising stock market. Last year the best stock market was Venezuela's, but try to buy something in a store on Main Street. Power goes out daily there. Caracas is one of the most violent cities in the world. Since all these people went to the same schools, I might begin to wonder about what is being taught there.

So much for capitalism. Bailing out banks, the purchase of junk bonds, and the manipulation of interest rates by the Fed is not capitalism. We all know the lobbyists are shady but what about the SEC who are making money front running- trading before the public on insider information.

Princeton and Northwestern Universities conducted a study in early 2014 that found "The U.S. government does not represent the interests of the majority of the country's citizens, but is instead ruled by those of the rich and powerful." If that were not the case, how do you explain politicians coming to Washington worth a few hundred thousand dollars, earning a few hundred thousand per year and leaving with millions? They do it by front running. Having access to inside information because they are working on that particular issue or done a favor for someone and gotten a reward in return.

Why is all this unfairness allowed? Asked and answered. Because they make the rules and you don't. You cannot get around them. They are the people you complain to about themselves.

Politicians are cleaver enough to use threats and bribery to scare the public into voting for them. The Feds are either so corrupt or so ignorant they won't even admit there is a problem. Probably just looking out for their own agenda. As one small example, who among us would believe that inflation is only 2%? Just because gas is down over the last few months means nothing. Gas was 29 cents in 1965. Hamburger was 80 cents, Cars cost $2500. I hate to even document the increase in health care and education costs.

In addition to the fact that you can't believe a word the government says, even if you did you would have to realize that unemployment is dropping because people are simply dropping out of the equation. The have given up and are no longer counted. Although the Shadow Statistics come up with some pretty good real numbers, it really hard to say exactly how many people are unemployed in some fashion. In addition to those mentioned above that have given up and are not counted, there are those who are underemployed, and let us not forget those who are gaming the system by claiming some bogus disability or living off alimony to the tune of $20,000 per month. Although according to government consumption theory, these deadbeats are shopping the hell out of the system and should be given a medal. Also, while passing around unsubstantiated information, is it possible that nearly half of Americans have less than $800 to their name? Things are more top heavy now than at any time since the robber baron times of the early 1900s.

CHAPTER FIVE - WAR

"Kill one man and you are a murderer, kill a million you are a conqueror, kill them all and you are a God" (Rostand, 1938).

We have become war mongers – Bush, Obama etc., "preemptive" wars are the norm, or merely opportunistic wars - they all seem to end up in misery and regret. As Bismarck put it, "it is like committing suicide for fear of death." (Bonner, 2006) Again, no wonder normal people dislike academics. A guy just wrote a book espousing his theory that Wars are good and necessary. Somehow a big one now and then prevents more of the same. The theory goes on and on but is so speculative as to reaffirm my theory that, if true, is just sad and if not, as humans we just bounce from dumb move to dumb move. To be fair, academics line up at the dumb trough just behind the military. I want to say only the high ranking career war mongers are at fault, but I have also met some pretty stupid lemming like eighteen year olds with "all the wrong moves". And they're the ones who get killed.

Remember when Dick Chaney said Deficits don't matter? Wrong Dicky! If a rapidly growing economy imports capital goods for the production of finished goods, perhaps it would be OK in the short run. This for the same reason that some really successful companies go broke because the over-run their money supply. They have to pay for their supplies and labor while waiting for the sales to be paid. Sometimes the sales take 90 days to be paid. In the interim you are cash poor. The more successful you are the faster this cycle is and the more you get behind cash wise. No credit line or deep pockets and you go out in a blaze of glory. As to the trade deficit, it can't be Gucci bags, toys and perfume. A deficit must lead somehow to an increase in household income and a higher standard of living. Study after study has indicated that incomes are not keeping up with the cost of living and most Americans are not doing as well as their parents did. Credit debt is up to hide these figures so much as to not bother to put down the numbers. Even if by some stretch the averages were up as to the increased standard of living, hat has been addressed often as flawed mathematics. Whatever gains in household wealth shown in averages have been unevenly distributed. Asset increases especially, usually leads to an enormous widening of wealth and income inequity. Look around you. Isn't that exactly what is happening? Chaney also made the remark that we should be spending our hard earned money on war rather than food stamps and highways (Bendery, 2014). That's the kind of person we have running our government. This would be a good time to jump forward to the discussion on sociopaths/psychopaths. Those same psychos found in corporations and Wall Street are not without a presence in government.

We were warned by one of their own. General Dwight D. Eisenhower repeatedly warned us not to allow the Military Industrial Complex to get into a position to control things. (Watts, 2009)

Funding the Iraq war, in hindsight, was a mistake. The Republicans were the warmongering cause; the Democrats being too busy investigating baseball players for steroids. Don't forget that when they did pay attention, the Democrats created the Fairness in Lending Laws which allowed greedy bankers to go nuts in the first place.

A lot of the world hates the Americans. Part of that is envy; it's easy to hate those who have more. It is probably justified. They hate us because we are lucky. We have natural resources. They could/should hate the oil producers for the same reason. It's certainly not for our system of government or the way we handle it.

War is costly. Think how much more good could be done with that money spending it on social issues. Instead of thinking in terms of a "military Industrial Complex" number like a 3% reduction, think in terms of a 70% reduction in the military budget. That would still put us ahead of everyone else in the world.

Why do governments do what they do – even when it is unproductive, expensive and dangerous? Because there are amoral bullies out there and because our government is one of them. You need me on that wall! Ourah! (The battle cry of the marines). Certain people in power just want an excuse to go to war or cause trouble.

Depending on who's figures you believe, during WWII, the Russia lost up to 8 million fighting men and another 12 million civilians. (New World Encyclopedia, 2015) Regardless, that's a lot of dead people

America should get out of the empire business. We are not very good at it. Somehow, we forgot to charge for it. We open the world to "free trade," and then lose market share. We celebrate our superiority, while the whole world laughs at us. (Bonner, 2006). Now our police have become just like the military. Who wants to be around a "tough cop?" I understand why they might have to be that way, but that doesn't make them any more pleasant. Same for the nastiness of spoiled actors, singers, athletes. They expect to get their own way.

War is not noble. It's not good, and it's not glorious, it's not a way out of recession and it's not productive; and anyone with any feeling, brains or maturity knows this. But if you denounce this game in any way they insinuate that you're a traitor. You know, "if you're not with me, you're against me. Wars drain an economy! The cost of bullets is never recovered. As an aside, notice none of the rich little boys or girls go off to die. That last applies mostly to inequality.

War benefits only two groups: Extremists and defense contractors. All at the expense of "heroes". The Generals want war because it's profitable. We really need to eliminate or control the Military Industrial complex. As a government we might want to learn how to respond to Terrorism.

Since when is being a vain bully such as Alexander, Napoleon, Mao, and Hitler a good thing?

What if we have another conventional war? We have no manufacturing left.

The Siege of Leningrad

3 million dead just here. (Andrews, 2014). But you weren't there, were you? You didn't see the dead frozen bodies of your best friend- just before he was cannibalized. That's OK though because some fat cat bureaucrat, congressman, lobbyist, general or white house aide wants a war so they can make some money, look good and maybe get ahead in their career. Besides, it's not expensive or dangerous for them. By the by, how in the world did the Germans lose Stalingrad, and what is the lesson to be learned? They were better equipped, better trained, accomplished their goal of occupying 90% of the city. Upon surrendering the German generals were killed. Right or wrong? Wrong by any surrendering standards, but right by what the Germans had done to them?

It takes two to tango is the expression. In the case of democracy there are the rich elites and the rest of us. The elites plan how to get what's best for them and we respond emotionally (because it is tough and we don't really understand what's going on. We have our daily lives to contend with. Besides, it wouldn't do any good anyway since we really can't influence policy.)

Was what Hitler did wrong? Certainly. But isn't all war wrong? In light of the Weimar Republic, the treatment at the Treaty of Versailles, huge inflation, country in shambles looking for a little pride (not withstanding that Prussian attitude, German arrogance and obstinacy), hard workers, cultured people; he was obviously the right man at the right time. Remember the Japanese, Attila the Hun, Genghis Chan, Caesar Alexander the Great. Why do we admire them, and not Hitler? Because he lost the war and the winners write history. Some say by a Jewish controlled press. Don't know. Did he look like a fanatic? Not really, except when he opened his mouth.

As a government we need to re-evaluate our plan to be the super-power to the world. It's expensive as well as egotistical. Curing the ego may take a while, but how come we are not charging to be the policemen of the world? That may be one of the reasons that as socialistic as the Europeans are, whether good or bad, they certainly can afford to do more for their people because they don't have the military expense the United States does.

Should we even be in places like Iraq and Afghanistan, and if so, go in and do the job- just like Viet Nam- stop playing with white gloves.

Even if you are anti-war you must protect yourself- you can't reason with unreasonable people.

For all our blow hard attitude, we don't seem to want or be able to do anything about North Korea. Now they have hacked the computers of a major corporation. Some say that is an act of war. I think we could come up with any number of reasons to annihilate them. Is it because we still believe we are the chosen ones and can't kill innocent people? After so much grief you as the population have to take some responsibility. Same thing with Cuba. How are they still in existence? I guess that means the Germans were responsible for Hitler to some extent.

Ron Paul has a good handle on one of our Empire attitude problems. He recently said that the military-security industry had Congress in its pocket. Because of that, he continued, we can expect more borrowing, more spending and more pointless and futile wars. They may be bad for the country and its citizens, says Paul, but they are good for the people who make fighter jets and combat fatigues. "We've been at war in the Middle East for decades," he said. "We supported Osama bin Laden against the Soviets in Afghanistan... and the result of that was the creation of AL-Qaeda. We supported Saddam Hussein against Iran. Saddam and bin Laden hated each other. But after 9/11 we attacked Saddam, using a bunch of lies to justify it. We sent over military equipment worth hundreds of billions of dollars. This equipment is now in the hands of ISIS – another enemy we created. (Bonner, 2014)

The United States has a military that is larger than the next ten countries combined, including China, a nation 4 or 5 times larger than us. (Suderman, 2014) Along with all than physical meanness we have a snoopy and data recording government that would make Ayn Rand and George Orwell roll over in their graves. In the name of security and protection from the bad guys our government is really loving the Big Brother role. Much of the money spent is going down a rat hole, the very nature of the operation breeds a type of person that should make your skin crawl (think a pretty boy from an ivy league school with a know it all attitude or an I know but can't tell you attitude. Smug, arrogant, evil, human beings. There is little worse than someone who is self-righteous and actually believes their right to push us around is God given. Not sure who's God is doing the giving. TV doesn't help this image either. Just watch any detective show. We claim we can annihilate any enemy with the stroke of our mighty sword, yet we can't beat a group of rag tag guys in Syria with pop guns driving around in the middle of nowhere and we are told they are an imminent threat. Please!

In Vietnam the big toughies and richies (us) again spend trillions fighting absolute nobodies for 13 years - and lost.

We spent trillions on Iraq and Afghanistan, both military lightweights. How cool is that that the most expensive and over-equipped military in the world can't beat up the local street corner gang.

Manipulation is standard operating procedure for the government. It would bring a tear to the eye of corporate executives. Some of us actually call that lying.

Fear-mongering is a great tool. You either buy into it or simply want to make money. War makes money.

The best way to describe the art of making war, and I use the word art very humorously, is to call it a complete sham. Especially those fought today. It seems painfully clear to one so average that we are being taken to the cleaners. There is generally no reason to enter into the conflict, and once we are there, we never use the strength we have to win; we just play at it in order to spend money and keep the military industrial complex in Bon Bons.

People go to war over food and energy. How come we didn't do that when we were getting it stuck to us? Actually maybe that's exactly what we are doing in the Middle East. I can't imagine any other reason for us to be there.

Even though it is a pipe dream, should you be able to trust people and countries, you would be able to eliminate and save the money on things like security, verification, audits, police, courts, surveillance, lawyers and other costs of protection and enforcement. Good luck on getting the Military Industrial Complex to go along with that.

The Austro-Hungarian Empire

Take a look at the First World War. A bang up job there. The 85 year old Austro-Hungarian Emperor made nine demands on the Serbians. Serbia met eight of his demands. They missed one out of nine in a decent effort. Didn't matter. Clearly the Austro-Hungarians wanted a war. Millions of people got killed. Bureaucrats always say the war will be over by Christmas (Kelly, 2015). Every war will be over by Christmas.. Billions of dollars get lost. Tell me again how war can help an economy? Usually no one can even tell you why one starts. In this case it was all because of one old man and the usual bureaucrats.

Military Industrial Complex

Former Vice President Dick Cheney has no regrets. "I believed in it then," Cheney told Politico's Mike Allen. "I look back on it now, it was absolutely the right thing to do" (Wofford, 2014)? In 2013, discretionary defense spending was $626 billion, or 3.8 percent of GDP, according to the Congressional Budget Office. For reference, that's more than China, Russia, Saudi Arabia, France, the U.K., Germany, Japan and India combined. The totality of the Bush administration's failure in Iraq is stunning. It is not simply that they failed to build the liberal democracy they wanted. It's that they ended up strengthening theocracies they feared (Bendery, 2014).

And it's not simply that they failed to find the weapons of mass destruction that they worried could one day be passed onto terrorists. It's that a terrorist organization now controls a territory about the size of Belgium, raising the possibility that America's invasion and occupation inadvertently trained the fighters and created the vacuum that will lead to AL Qaeda's successor organization. And all this cost us trillions of dollars and thousands of American lives.

CHAPTER SIX - MONEY AND BANKING

There are so many ways the commercial banks and Wall Street are cheating us it's hard to know where to start.

Central banks lend to insider banks and their buddies at rates below inflation. And yet, even with the ridiculously cheap money, bankers still manage to lose money, after paying big bonuses of course. Besides, if and when they get in trouble and go broke, the Fed will be there to bail them out. How can you lose money when all you are doing is giving the money right back to the government without any risk? Even if you don't go broke that is hardly a management plan to be rewarded with bonuses. A monkey could do that. Sometimes these bankers actually work against the Fed's game plan, first by not lending to business ventures and secondly by speculating and driving up asset prices. Well, I guess the asset bubbles are what the government wants come to think about it, but higher food and energy prices sure don't help the average worker any. None of this provides any worthwhile job, mind you.

Why in the world do government wonks do what they do? Are they crazy? Probably not. Greedy and self-serving yes, but in most cases, they actually have an explanation/justification for what they do.

Some actually believe in what they do. How long can a government perpetrate a hoax? Don't know, we'll see. With that in mind we should be aware of inflation's country cousin, Keynesian Economics.

Savings, unless put under a mattress, goes to the banks who re-lend it to businesses and entrepreneurs (or should). Banks don't pay interest on funds deposited so that they can sit on the money. 2014 banking procedures being the exception thanks to giving it back to Uncle Sam.

By reducing the interest rate at which the central bank lends money to commercial banks, lowering the reserve requirements or buying bonds, the government puts money into the economy and sends a signal to commercial banks that they pass those benefits along to their customers. Of course, as we all know, the banks didn't play fair the last time around and they hoarded the money.

Then there is always the self-perpetuating risk; if wages and prices were falling, people would start to expect them to fall. This could make the economy spiral downward as those who had money would simply wait as falling prices made it more valuable – rather than spending. Deflation (falling prices) can make a depression deeper as falling prices and wages made pre-existing nominal debts more valuable in real terms. That's true for inflation as well. As asked and answered often, renegotiate the debt also!

Unsold goods and materials encourages businesses to decrease both production and employment. This in turn lowers people's incomes – and saving. For Keynes, the fall in income did most of the job by ending excessive saving. Instead of interest-rate adjustment solving the problem, a recession does.

A recession undermines the business incentive to engage in plant and equipment. With falling incomes and demand for products, the desired demand for factories and equipment (not to mention housing) will fall. This recreates the problem of excessive saving and encourages the recession to continue. It would be Classical, free market thinking to allow the recession, not Keynesian.

Paul Volker restricted the money supply and tamed inflation. So, in this case, monetarism worked for fighting inflation. It didn't address unemployment but, the term "stagflation" meant both inflation and unemployment were high.   Was it the wise course of action to give virtually free money to the banks to make them whole again? What would have happened if they had been allowed to fail? Nothing. Just shareholders, bondholders, management all wiped out, depositors protected and a new beginning.   Banks are set up to take substantial risks. They invest in assets with longer maturities and get the funds to do so from unsophisticated, uninformed and fully insured depositors. Therefore, there is no way depositors can, or even want to, take the time to discipline them. Add to that a self-interested rational, tremendous leverage, and a minuscule chance of major consequences or getting caught and the formula not only spells disaster but it totally unfair. Stir in a pinch of lobbying and the stew is set to boil over.

Profits can be obtained while taking a social enhancement posture. Are you telling me that here is an industry that can't exist by providing services at a reasonable price without committing crimes in order to stay in business?

David Ricardo said that as long as the Bank is willing to lend, borrowers will always exist, so that there is no practical limit to the over-issue of money. So, don't tell me you can't get the consumer to borrow and spend.

When times get tough and banks try to make up for their mistakes the rich get richer. So, the government makes the rich richer. Is there any hope for correcting this system? Banks tighten their credit standards far too much, forcing out not only the bad guys that deserve it but the average person who is trying to start a business or rehab a property legitimately. And they can justify this in their own minds and on paper because it is probable, although totally unnecessary, that the rich do not only have more assets but have better credit. Why wouldn't the rich have better credit? They don't have to scrimp and save, robbing Peter to pay Paul and doing without.

Thanks to the government through FHA, Freddie Mac or Fannie Mae, banks are no longer even banks, they are Mortgage Bankers who simply pass through loans to the secondary market. There are no more portfolio loans being made. The government has taken risk out of the equation for bankers.

The sad fact is that Quantitative easing went to the wrong people and didn't work There was no trickle down. Another great deal for bankers and Wall Street, but not for Main Street.

What risk would there be really to the government if the banks were put out of business? Only stockholders, bondholders and (definitely) executives would be wiped out, fired and put in jail. Yes, the government would be on the hook for some depositor money- but certainly a 100% hit! People would be brought in to replace them and life would go on.

If you or I went into a bank and asked that our home values be tripled so we could get an addition to our credit line, would we get it? Our excuse would be "I can't pay my bills and can't find a buyer so I have had to sell some furniture and one of the cars. The banker pretty much tells you to drop dead, for any number of reasons, good and bad. Later, the Banker goes to the Treasury and says, "I can't find a buyer for any of my mortgage backed assets and the margin calls are piling up. I've nearly had to sell one of the company jets." The Treasury says, we've decided to relax the rules...we're gonna let you revalue those smelly loans to whatever you want. And the beat goes on. I guess what's good for the goose is not good for the gander.

Today it seems the governments of the world have yet to learn the lessons of history. They're still trying to bail out everyone who they think can do them some good. Even bad ideas work for a while, but it's usually a temporary fix. It doesn't solve the structural defects. One defect is the addiction to debt. I am not willing to even concede that all those banks failing and Wall Street seizing up would have ended badly for the average person. On the surface it looked like the Feds solved the credit crunch by printing money.

Has anyone every laid out for you just how much money we're talking about? Here's a short list, by no means complete.

The U.S. government bellied up with $700 billion in TARP money for the banks. It has loaned, invested or committed $200 billion to nationalize the world's two largest mortgage companies, Fannie Mae and Freddie Mac, $25 billion for the Big Three auto manufacturers, $29 billion for Bear Stearns, $150 billion for AIG, $350 billion for Citigroup, $300 billion for the Federal Housing Administration Rescue Bill to refinance bad mortgages, $87 billion to pay back JP Morgan Chase for bad Lehman Brothers trades, $200 billion in loans to banks under the Fed's Reserve Term Auction Facility (TAF), $50 billion to support short-term corporate IOUs held by money market mutual funds, $500 billion to rescue various credit markets, $620 billion for industrial nations, including the Bank of Canada, Bank of England, Bank of Japan, National Bank of Denmark, European Central Bank, Bank of Norway, Reserve Bank of Australia, Bank of Sweden and the Swiss National Bank, $120 billion in aid for emerging markets, including the central banks of Brazil, Mexico, South Korea and Singapore, trillions to guarantee the FDIC's new, expanded bank deposit insurance coverage from $100,000 to $250,000, plus trillions more for other sweeping guarantees (Weiss, 2009a). Have you yet asked what in the world we were lending money to those other countries for?

Grand total: $7.8 trillion and counting. And that *excludes* any bailout for Detroit, a new $500 billion stimulus package expected soon, plus hundreds of billions for at least 19 states running out of money for unemployment benefits.

I can see justification for keeping car makers in business. But AIG? Why? Especially after the bonus fiasco. Talk about having friends in high places.

So why did we bother with that stupid TARP thing anyway? A lot of the banks now say that didn't even want TARP funding. Liars! The government FORCED them take the money...and then forced the top executives to get by on a $1 million per year. Poor baby. Just imagine; being forced to take a $10 billion loan from the government, along with tens of billions of additional low-interest loans and special guarantees. And then imagine the agony of drawing a paltry $1 million paycheck from a company that would have gone bankrupt without the government's help. It's been a horrible, horrible experience for all involved. Oh, woe is me. The too-big-to-fail scheme doesn't hurt attitudes either and further undermines any reasoning for large salaries and bonuses. It's still called hoarding and it's wrong! How can you not make money? Wait! They do actually spend some of the money on something other than themselves. They use some of it to bribe Congress. Special interests do and did just fine also. Oh yeah, and they re-lend the money back to the government. Thaaaaaaaats why the government gives them money.

If taxpayers support the banks, why in the world would the government think it was OK to use that money to pay bonuses- and allow it? The banks should be lending all the money to homeowners and small businesses. Fairness is a word rapidly being erased from the dictionary.

The only reason banks are in business is that the government is guaranteeing their entire operation. Their modus operandi is to take huge risks with monumental leverage so they can pay themselves obscenely and then when it all goes South whine to the government to bail them out. We know they're a bunch of stupid, inexperienced, fools and idiots or cleaver diabolical amoral rogues. What I can't figure out is why the government puts up with it.

Another pretty cool trick the banks have is they know they can't lose, lending money to third world countries, who can barely pay the interest let alone the principal, because the Federal Reserve guarantees that these loans that go into default will be covered by the Fed (you and me) because they're too big to fail. The game plan is to roll the loan over a few times, each time lending the poor country a little more to pay back interest and finally then, to reschedule the loan- meaning reduce the interest and extend the time frame. Ultimately, Uncle Sam steps in with the guarantee. Did I mention above that the guarantee is coming out of your pocket? Neat, huh?

The money printing of the Federal Reserve is providing an unintended support to the real estate market which benefits the rich primarily. Much of the money, in addition to the rich here in the United States, is coming from foreign buyers with a lot of cash thanks to the cheaper dollar policy of the government. So, how is that helping the average American again?

Thanks to taxpayer money, the bankers were allowed to make mistakes and pay themselves huge bonuses and then get bailed out. What's fair about that? The taxpayers aren't even upset about it because they either don't have a clue as to what is going on or just don't care. The bankers are going to complain, they're living high on the hog. I wish I were a banker.

There was and are all kinds of justification theories for spending money. More of that two sides to every story, depending on what you are out to prove. Much is discussed regarding the degeneration of money but mostly ignored. Too much incentive to keep printing. Illusions and delusions are powerful forces.

Self-righteous bureaucrats, whether in the government or in the banks, never tire of telling us how their mandate is to serve the public. I've heard of not reading your own press clippings but that's ridiculous.

Advocates of the rich and powerful having it all are quick to point to the conspiracy theories as proof that they are right and anything to the contrary is the work of the "Crazies". As usual, we exaggerate too much and that undermines our line of reason. I find it highly entertaining and actually want to believe some of it, but they do get carried away. There is usually a grain of truth in even the most outrageous story. But why exaggerate when the truth is bad enough? To think that all the questioning of whether something is wrong or not is false and the rich would not do bad things to others is equally foolish.

There is a big difference between conspiracy of the rich to rule and the silliness of psychic and occult fanaticism. With that in mind we should take a look at one sample of the mischief concocted by the power brokers and judge for ourselves.

The Creature from Jekyll Island.

That's the term given to our Federal Reserve System by G. Edward Griffin in his book by the same title. (Griffin, 1994). Oh, and it's not Federal, and it has no reserves.

As boondoggles go, this wasn't the first attempt. As bad ideas go, this one has been brewing for a long time. To get a better historical perspective on the formation of the Federal Reserve we have to start farther back. It is the fourth attempt at some kind of National Bank and all have ended badly before, usually with a lot of inflation and economic chaos. As good as the founding fathers were, they were not without detractors and different opinions.

From the very beginning good men have been against the idea. George Mason of Virginia: "I have a mortal hatred of paper money." John Langdon of New Hampshire: "I would rather reject the whole Constitution than grant the new government the right to issue fiat money." George Reed of Delaware: "The right to issue fiat money would be as alarming as the mark of the beast in Revelation." Thomas Paine: "The punishment of a member of Congress who should move for such a law ought to be death." (Griffin, 1994)

Alexander Hamilton was a Federalist, which for the most part was a good thing. Depending on where you stand on the issue though, he was for the National bank, and a reasonable debt carriage, although he did qualify his stance by saying "if not excessive". His side also felt that taxes would spur growth. On the opposing side was James Madison and Thomas Jefferson – against both a national bank and debt. The first attempt, in 1782, was the Bank of North America. This push was led by Robert Morris, who was Superintendent of Finance at the time. Next came the First National Bank of the United States in 1791- 1811, the effort headed by Alexander Hamilton. The Second National Bank of the United States came into being in 1816 with a twenty year charter. President Andrew Jackson was against this one (Charles, 2008). In 1863 they tried again, somewhat to finance the war effort and because of the wildcat state banks who were unreliable. You can imagine the problems that might occur when you have many different banks issuing their own currency. How in the world do you tell whether or not the money is legitimate and can be retrieved or will be honored by anyone else? What's it backed with?

Granted, there were problems in the 1800s in the banking industry. There were also efforts to cure the problems. There was some legitimate concern that something was needed to smooth out the ripples in the economy. Just what would do it and who would benefit is the quandary. Until our system changes for the better, those with the power and wealth are going to see to it that they have a say in it and get more than their fair share. The banking acts of 1863 and 1864 were on the right track. Some kind of national banking system was to be desired, a standardized national currency was a good idea, and some kind of secondary market was a good idea to move money around to where it was needed (Osterberg & Thomson, 1998). Even a temporary elasticity was a good idea- the key word being "temporary." It's fine to print money for a short while as long as you pay it back and tear it up.

Time passes. Speculation has it that the bankers deliberately caused the panic of 1907. They deliberately put the U.S. into a monetary crisis so they could come riding to the rescue and look like the good guys. In the interval they ruined people's lives. Were they justified or just corrupt and out for their own well-being?

We would all do well to remember that, like the inflation/deflation debates, the panic of 1907, as well as most others, was caused by previous greed and bad investments. The Knickerbocker Trust failure is yet another example of being assured by their management that all is well – right up until they decided to go bankrupt. F. Augustus Heinze's was trying to corner the stock of United Copper Company. He failed. No big deal except that failure exposed the interconnection of the people on the boards of many banks, especially in New York City, which began to make depositors nervous. (Moen & Tallman, The Bank Panic of 1907: The Role of the Trust Companies., 1992) Clearly, a run on a bank can be a problem without the ability to get temporary funds, so some kind of clearing house should be in place, like overnight bankers acceptances. It just shouldn't be financed by an individual like JP Morgan who holds the government hostage and extracts unfair profits.

Transportation of crops to the East Coast and on to Europe was financed by NY banks. Because there was less money, money was valuable and interest rates went up. Since interest rates were up investment money came in from Europe easing the lack of liquidity somewhat. This time the economy was slowing and the stock market was falling. Because of problems the English were having themselves, the normal inflow of gold was not happening. Farmers needed money in the spring to buy supplies so local banks borrowed some from NY banks. Farmers paid off loans at harvest in the fall so local banks had money. Where was the money they paid back to the NY banks then? That money should have been enough to finance shipping. (Moen & Tallman, The Bank Panic of 1907: The Role of the Trust Companies., 1992)

At the same time money was inelastic, therefore could not expand if need be. (Moen & Tallman, 2000) The question is, why should it need be? The money had to be somewhere. Even after national banks came into existence there remained the problem that the securities deposited with the government that determined how money could be in circulation depended on the market value of the bonds, not the par value. In any case, based on bonds rather than the needs of the economy. Therefore, if the securities went down in value money would have to be removed from circulation. That would appear to be a flaw to work on. That may have worked if the banks just stopped lending and allowed attrition to work but not when banks called in loans on demand (meaning without warning and immediately). If banks had a problem with runs because they had lent the money deposed out to others, wouldn't the same hold true for consumers who borrowed the money to use and not to just hold?

Many questions still remain unanswered regarding the panic. Did newspapers treat Wall Street favorably? Was the Panic of 1907 outside human control, or a human-induced crisis? Then there is the overriding question of whether or not JP Morgan and others may have profited by creating some of the problems and then lending money to otherwise desperate bankers and the government at stranglehold terms. (Sprague, 1910) What's wrong with the system when you allow the rich and powerful to control and run ruff shod over your government?

A critical issue we have here in the United States especially, but everywhere else as well, is how government is manipulated by a few wealthy and powerful people, and is that OK. Very few knowledgeable people have anything good to say about J.P. Morgan. It seems a consensus that he was not a nice man. No question he had the confidence (along with inherited money), was brash, a brute, a barbarian, intimidating, used force, used corrupt trickery and used strangleholds. It was profit at any cost. And profit and power there was. Morgan was responsible for the formation of General electric, which did get rid of soot and death by gas fumes, US Steel, which build ships (for commerce), Railroads, which did help to open up new territory for living and exploration of natural resources and the Panama Canal which shortened shipping time and saved money, for the rich I'm betting. But wouldn't all of that occur anyway regardless of who owned the entities? What was the trickle down percentage for the average person? Meanwhile working hours increased and workplace fatalities increase. Morgan also participated heavily in the formation, (through raising money usually) of AT & T, International Harvester, Case, Atlas Portland Cement and many others.

He was another Donald Trump type, having inherited Daddy's money for a big leg up to start. Morgan did fail several times but that only proves it's hard to lose all the money Daddy left you if you have infinite chances. "While some multimillionaires robber barons started in poverty, most did not. A study of the origins of 303 textile, railroad and steel executives of the 1870s showed that 90% came from middle or upper class families." (Zinn, 1980)

How did he do it? Putting companies together, bailing out companies- all of which takes a group of investors. The process of creating a monopoly through the elimination of competition and the maximization of profits by slashing the workforce and reducing their wages is named after JP Morgan. It was called

Morganization. Morgan was another of the typical rich who escaped military service during the Civil War by paying $300 to a substitute to fight for him. During the war he buys five thousand rifles at $3.50 each and sells them on at $22 apiece. The rifles are defective and some shoot off the thumbs of the soldiers firing them. (Zinn, 1980) Don't see much of that in the history books.

In Morgan's battle with George Westinghouse, Morgan used his enormous wealth to force Westinghouse to sign over Tesla's patents. Money talks. At the same time he pushed Edison out of the company. Not a nice man. Morgan and his cronies were so powerful their money bought the election of 1896 simply by outspending their opponent by 5 to 1. Plus voting was a more public affair and workers know they may be fired if seen to be voting for the opponent. If you think no harm is done by such men, sadly recall that the man who shot President McKinley was a factory worker who lost his job in a JP Morgan takeover. (Zinn, 1980)

Interestingly, Morgan controlled the White Star Shipping Line, owner of the Titanic. He was supposed to be on that infamous voyage. Some people might view that as proof that there really is no justice.

In 1910, partially as a result of the 1907 Panic, on Jekyll Island off the coast of Georgia a coalition of Wall Street bankers and U.S. Senators met. Those in attendance were: Senator Nelson Aldrich, Frank Vanderlip of National City (today know as Citibank), Henry Davison of J.P. Morgan Bank, A. Piatt Andrew

Assistant Sec of the Treasury, Charles Norton (president of Morgan's First National Bank), Benjamin Strong (president of Morgan's Bankers Trust Co.) and Paul Warburg of the Kuhn, Loeb Investment House. The meeting was held in secret because the participants knew that any plan they generated would be rejected automatically in the House of Representatives if it were associated with Wall Street. (Griffin, 1994) Ya think! Depending on your point of view, the bankers wanted to establish a new central bank under the direct control of New York's financial elite so they could manipulate it for their personal gain (the Federal Reserve Act gave control of the banking system to the money trusts), or, the intent was to take control away from them. (Griffin, 1994)

The operation of the Federal Reserve is sometimes referred to as the Mandrake Mechanism, which is defined as the method by which the Federal Reserve creates money out of nothing; the payment of interest on pretended loans. The name comes from a comic strip character from the 1940s called Mandrake the Magician who could create things out of nothing.

Is the money created first, is the money created from debt, or is it not created until borrowed? The latter would have some basis today, as the banks have received the money but are not lending it out.

Fodder for another discussion is whether or not there is any reserve ratio at all when the stuff used as reserves isn't really money but bought Treasury bonds, which are a debt; so talk of "reserve ratios" is a moot point.

They admitted that they wanted to stop competition. Not that I totally disagree, due to the wildcat banking that was going on, but isn't competition supposed to be good? In the same vein they admitted to wanting to control all the reserves. I guess for the same reason. They admitted to wanting to create dollars- for excuses discussed many times along with the reasons it's a bad idea. The no accountability thing is a two edged sword of course.

Perhaps they just realized, unlike the rich of today, that one might want to be a little less greedy and leave scraps for others, else the others might get mad a kill you. No doubt some measure of control was necessary due to so many state banks issuing their own currency and then going belly up. Plus the big New York banks did have a lot of control. Following the return to central banking, at least some measure of control was removed from them and placed with the Federal Reserve. This is a little naïve since they did meet at Jekyll Island, and why would they do that if not for their own gain? The formation of the Federal Reserve certainly didn't hurt the bankers. More would have to be researched to determine if the appointment of Paul Warburg as the first Chairman of the Fed was a good idea because he was qualified, or because he was one of the inner group of bankers.

"These plotters were already affiliated with the conspiratorial British one world Round Table Group, The Round Table was a group founded and headed by Cecil Rhodes, known for his Rhodes scholarship, yet not so well known for being a ruthless, devious, lying, cheating scoundrel. The United States followed with its own version of corruption with the Council on Foreign Relations here in the US." (Griffin, 1994) That might be a bit stiff regarding any tie in to corruption on the part of the CFR. Remember, a grain of truth in the most outrageous lie. Then Congress became either the lap dogs or a part of the conspiracy by passing this unconstitutional act creating the perfect insider's toy, a central bank with the ability to inflate. Griffin also insinuates that the International Monetary Fund and the World Bank are also stooges for those in power used to create world-wide inflation. (Griffin)

Treasury IOUs (bonds) are converted by the Federal Reserve into money through the issuance of Federal Reserve checks, with no money in existence to cover them, which the Fed then uses to buy the Treasury bonds. I did this and I would go to jail. "Congress has made this legal for the Fed, however, because this hidden process allows our congressmen to enjoy unlimited revenue without having to visibly raise taxes." (Griffin, 1994) This still begs the question of how long can it go on?

Fractional Banking System

To see this degeneration of money in action and a justification for it, look no further than the Fractional Reserve Banking system whereby banks can expand the money supply. Every time money is loaned out it gets redeposited somewhere else and can be relent-minus whatever reserve requirements are in place at the time. Assume a reserve requirement of 20%, which is really high, for simplicity. Starting with $100 in deposit at Bank A, that bank makes a loan of $80 and puts $20 in reserve. The person receiving the loan (borrower 1) buys something with the money and that recipient then puts the $80 in his bank. His bank (bank B) lends out 80% or $64 and places $16 in reserves. That borrower (2) pays for something and his seller takes the money to his bank. Bank C lends out $51.20 and places $12.80 in reserves. Borrower 3 pays for something and that recipient deposits the funds in his bank. His bank (bank D) lends $40.96 to borrower 4 who pays for something which gets deposited into the recipient's bank (E) who lends out $32.77 to borrower 5. That borrower paid someone for something and the recipient deposited the funds into his bank which lent out $26.22 putting the rest in reserves. So we started with, and still have, only $100- yet somehow there is $395.15 in use. Welcome to Fractional Banking. With a more realistic reserve of around 3 to 5% the lending scam is exacerbated.

Back in 1931 the argument (the bank-deposit theory of prices) was advanced that deposits were not cash deposited by customers but were created by the banks by granting loans, thereby creating a credit, which somehow becomes a deposit (Werner, 2015). Our boy Keynes was at the heart of that draft as well. When you get a handle on that one let me know, it's obviously beyond me. It's a little disturbing to think these people are that much smarter than I am. This doctrine somehow eventually evolved into Fractional Banking.

If you could believe their suggested hypothesis, then individuals lending among themselves would not increase the money stock, while if given to a bank which re-lent it, would allow the fractional banking to take effect and the money would be multiplied by nine. Based on a 10% reserve.

Edwin Cannan, at the University of London, in referring to what he called the bank-deposit theory of prices, said, economists believe the interest bankers pay should be counted as part of total currency, are wrong. He also said, "With the exception of a small amount of currency which they keep ready to meet any demands by customers, the banks have paid away money as they receive it, spending a little on buildings in order to conduct their business, and investing or lending all the rest. The other side rejected Cannan's idea that deposits in banks are cash deposited by customers, and argued that: The bulk of the deposits arise out of the action of the banks themselves, for by granting loans, allowing money to be drawn on overdraft ... a bank creates a credit in its books which is the equivalent of a deposit. (Cannan, 1931) Does that sound like the way the system was supposed to work to you?

Is it possible that the system is even more inflated than this would indicate? Even before other banks get involved, we make the mistake of thinking in terms of only keeping $10 in for the $100 deposit while lending out $90. In reality, the entire $100 could be kept in the bank and therefore $900 can be lent out. My math may be a little shaky but isn't that, not 9-10 times the amount, but 90 to 100 times the actual amount of cash? A factor of 10 times a factor of 10 would be a 100 times fractional banking system. Oops. Feel free to contradict me.

The government doesn't seem to be doing a very good job of monitoring Wall Street. Even as recently as the Enron scandals, somebody went to jail. Skip forward a mere decade or two. Merrill Lynch revealed a $7.9 billion loss on sub-prime bets in 2007, they fired their CEO, Stanley O'Neal, and gave him *$161.5 million* as he exited the door. Ex-Citigroup CEO Chuck Prince, walked with $140 million while scratching his head as to where they had lost around $17 million (Sorkin, 2010). Would this be a good place to remind you that a mere 3-5% drop in assets at the astounding leverage these guys are using would make them bankrupt. Someone should tell Uncle Sam this doesn't send a very good message to the public. Blood and Circuses, guys.

Morgan Stanley, J.P. Morgan, Bank of America, Bear Sterns, Goldman Sachs etc. It's a who's who of the screw your neighbor crowd. Don't forget, right after paying the big bonuses, thousands of employees will get laid off. As they are walking out the door with their bonuses these Ivy League B school shysters freely admit they have no clue why this all happened or what will happen next. Even in the land of austerity, the stalwart German bank, Deutsche Bank, had sub-prime related losses of $3.1 billion

(Sorkin, 2010). As mentioned in addressing Dick Fuld at Lehman; are these congressmen just not as smart as Wall Street. Probably not. Nevertheless, just put your foot down. How tough can it be?

Why are bank stocks down after the Fed decided not to raise rates? Because banks make more money in a high rate environment. The spread between what the banks pay depositors and the price at which they can lend out money is narrower when rates are low. That means they can only stick it to you a little. Bonuses don't reduce however. There's no reason to believe (and no proof) that what's good for bankers is good for America. (Krugman, The Rage of Bankers, 2015) They are also supposed to be experts on the economy, but nothing in history supports that belief either. (Krugman, The Rage of Bankers)

Reserve Currency and Risk Aversion

No doubt being the Reverse Currency is a big advantage. There is no checks and balance on us. We are the only country that can print at will in theory without a ceiling. When the world panics, the United States dollar usually rallies. US bonds also rally. It's not that there is any quality associated with us, we are just the best apple in a bad barrel. Our economy is large and liquid. That's called risk aversion. Beats me why money wouldn't flood into Germany or Norway. Stocks and commodities have a tendency to fall when the dollar strengthens. Of course, with Uncle Sam keeping low interest rates and stimulating the economy, normal behavior goes out the window as stocks go up in spite of the strong dollar.

China is definitely dumping dollars whenever possible, and certainly wants our reign as reserve currency to end. As does Russia. Those are two worthy foes, economically and even militarily. Mark my words, after those two make their deals with each other, they will then start on other Asian countries, the Middle East, South America and Africa. Come to think of it, just who is on our side?

Goldman Sachs ~~owns~~ IS the Government

No doubt when you think of who manipulated the government best you think of Goldman Sachs. There is little question that these are brilliant people. I picture herding them underground every so often like the Morlocks did the Eloi. I'm sure they're delicious.

How come the government allows Goldman Sachs to pay outrageous bonuses and commit fraud?

It gets worse. Just like our poor attempts at empire building, we aren't even that good at capital allocation either. Wall Street claims to be using its derivatives and other complicated products to make the economy safer while speeding up growth. It says it's the best at raising and allocating capital. Allocating capital to its highest, most efficient uses is what makes an economy grow so the capitalism primer says, right? So, how is it possible that people who just discovered capitalism 20 years ago could do a better job of it than Harvard grads motivated by million-dollar bonuses?

How could a smart guy, with the best financial education that money could buy, with hundreds of years of capitalism behind him, backed by a government that professes to want to help him and flanked by almost unlimited capital, technology, and expertise, fall right on his face? How can the Chinese under the cloak of Communism beat us at our own game while growing their capital base 10 times faster?

Human nature being what it is, let's not forget the other half. A nurse at the VA hospital sadly spoke about the deadbeats who didn't deserve the benefits because they were cheaters and even then they felt they were entitled, all he while being rude and impolite.

Again to be fair, you don't have to be a rocket scientist in economics to notice that government interference does seems to muck up an economy. When private businesses are not allowed to fire employees that may breed complacency. Truth be told there is a large unemployment rate in the socialist European countries. When "going on the dole" becomes a part of your five year plan so you can goof off at government expense there may be a problem there.

Economist Jeffrey Sachs observed "that among developed countries, those with high rates of taxation and high social welfare spending perform better on most measures of economic performance compared to countries with low rates of taxation and low social outlays. He concludes that Friedrich Hayek was wrong to argue that high levels of government spending harms an economy, and "a generous social-welfare state is not a road to serfdom but rather to fairness, economic equality and international competitiveness." (Sachs, 2006) Others like Austrian school economist Sudha Shenoy countered by claiming that "countries with large public sectors have grown more slowly." (Shenoy, 2009) Again, is growth the best benchmark for success?

Every fifth paragraph I do my best to emphasize that the average American continues to fall behind economically, while those at the very top are doing extraordinarily well. That's according to the government's own income data. I also say as often as possible that Washington is in cahoots with the wealthy.

Nouriel Roubini said, "This recent financial turmoil is the beginning of a much more serious and protracted U.S. and global credit crunch (Thomas, 2007). The risks of a systemic crisis are rising: Liquidity injections and lender-of-last-resort bailout of insolvent borrowers -- however necessary and unavoidable during a liquidity panic -- will not work; they will only postpone and exacerbate the eventual and unavoidable insolvencies."

Being allowed to leverage at 33 to 1, with other people's money, simply lie about fat profits that will come from unfathomable financial products, and stuff your own pockets with big bonuses is probably not capitalism as any of the economic thinkers of the past would suggest. Yet they got bailed out. What happens when fiscal irresponsibility gets rewarded with bailouts? You get more fiscal irresponsibility.

Knowing that the Feds will be there to bail them out, the banks will continue to take more risk. As long as this expectation remains, financial bubbles will occur again and again. The current credit bubble will burst – someday

Another wrinkle in today's scenario is, now everyone is doing it. "Gee, if some folks are not paying their mortgages and are going to get bailed out, why shouldn't I? The little folk are wising up, thanks to the internet. I have a feeling the crooks didn't count on that. Only so much room in the boat, you know.

Thomas Friedman once said, "The current debate about work going to India, China and Mexico is actually no different from the debate once held about submarine work leaving New London or shoe work leaving Massachusetts or textile work leaving North Carolina. Work gets done where it can be done most effectively and efficiently...it helps because it frees up people and capital to do different, more sophisticated work (like what, and how come that ain't happening?) and it helps because it gives an opportunity to produce the end product more cheaply, benefiting customers even as it helps the corporation." (Friedman, 2005) What a total moron. No doubt it helps those at the top of the corporations because it is produced more cheaply, but the cheapness to the customer means nothing because they don't have a job. What about that, Tommy?

He goes on to use the disappearance of the buggy whip as an example of why we shouldn't worry about the auto industry disappearing from America.

First of all one would wonder just why the brightest and best here in America can't build a decent car at a profit. Besides, the difference is that the buggy whip was replaced with more work in the auto industry. What is replacing the auto industry now? But we still have automobiles. Even the Germans and the Japanese can do a good job in a high wage environment. Innovation used to bring increased wages. Now all the profit goes to executives. Because Capitalism has become corrupt, Washington now, as opposed to two centuries ago, consists of scoundrels, liars, crooks and self-serving blunderbuss who play the system for their own benefit. Wall Street plays everyone for chumps, including Washington. The pay is great too. Meanwhile the investors want their little piece of the action immediately so they are guilty also. Normally managers are not really capitalists. They're just greedy humans who don't care about anybody but themselves. Gee, I guess they are capitalists. What I meant was they are not leaders in the sense that they share in the profits. Therefore they must do all they can to get it while they can like the rest of us, only sooner. At no level does anyone want to work for anything. Just gimme something for nothing...as soon as possible. The unions want their benefits. The executives want their bonuses or golden parachutes. Investors want the share price to rise. Nobody cares about a long term business.

American democracy has lasted for 250 years-is that a good test time? What about the Greeks? They were finally ousted by barbarians because they became soft. Was that the only thing? Same with the Romans. Have things changed so being the bully doesn't carry the same weight? Does democracy have a finite end? Is it a foregone conclusion or is there hope for a reprieve? If so, why and when? Is it possible that as one becomes wealthier, more liberal and egalitarian that the system becomes loaded down with bureaucracy? If so, shame on us as humans. That doesn't give much hope for the future and leaves the conservatives with too little fault.

Past recessions were triggered by monetary tightening, the Fed's response to rising inflation rates. Consistent with tight credit, consumers and businesses slashed their credit-financed expenditures. These were the same components in all economic downturns - consumer durables, business investment and residential building.

The downturn of 2001 was unlike other recessions. It was the first recession to happen under conditions of rampant credit expansion.

So what do you think causes these bubbles? I guess booming consumption and financial speculation.

Honestly, there are well educated economists who actually believe the United States is able to evolve into some new kind of economy, made up of service only- no manufacturing, interest toys peddled by Wall Street and communication that really does nothing economical. This new wonder world can handle far higher debt loads, people can live in bigger houses with bigger mortgages and the trade deficit really doesn't matter. For an old plodder like me that just doesn't sound right. Incomes per hour are not going up. Wives had to go to work. The only profits going up, or even breaking even, seem to be from selling iPods or making movies.

We are a nation of service companies using other peoples' labor. We also have no "cheap"oil and very few skills. On the other hand the average worker had it good for a very long time had he/she been a union worker working for an auto company.

How can anyone possibly think that an economy that has grown because of government spending and accumulation of massive public and private debts is going to, one day, magically, be transformed into one that does NOT depend on government spending and ever-higher debt loads? Then where is the money going to come from, moron?

Will we fail as a society? When? In a year-five years-100 years? Just because it isn't going to fail in the short run doesn't mean it won't fail or isn't on the wrong path. Or that it is a success. There is strong evidence to suggest that democracies has a finite life. Think of Greece, Rome, Britain, and Spain. Even China in the distant past.

If the dollar is not a safe haven but people think it is, what do you do? Is perception everything?

Bond pricing and deliberate inflation

A public and private debt-to-GDP ratio above the range of 260-275% depresses economic growth. From 1871 to 1999, private and public debt averaged less than 165% of GDP (well below the 260-275% critical level), and growth in real GDP was 3.8%. From 2000 through 2013, GDP growth has been around 1.9%. Why? Because total private and public debt was 344% of GDP. (Reinhart, Reinhart, & Rogoff, 2012)

According to the Organization for Economic Cooperation and Development (OECD), the public ratio reached 104.1% in 2013, the highest level since the early 1950s. Europe's is 106.4%. History says these levels hinder growth, only get worse, and last for decades. These numbers are the worst they have been since 1826 (Reinhart, Reinhart, & Rogoff, 2012)

Quantitative easing by the Federal Reserve is quite possibly slowing economic activity.

Real interest rates

This level determines the price of credit. In 2013, long-term Treasury bond yields rose 100 basis points, or 1.0%. The inflation rate dropped 50 basis points. This pushed the real yield on the 30-year bond to nearly 3% at the close of 2013. Thus, real yields currently carry a significant premium to the long-term average. All of this ties to the Fisher equation which says real interest rates are determined by subtracting the inflation rate from the nominal (actual) rate. (Hoisington & Hunt, 2014) Example: 30 year nominal bond yield of 4.5% minus inflation of 2% equals a real rate of return of 2.5%. While inflation and bond yields fluctuate, the real yield has stayed about the same. Over long periods, the real yield has stayed around its post-1871 average of 2.2%. Therefore, when inflation is low, real rates will be lower also.

Banks have what they call a money multiplier (the conversion of bank reserves into deposits). A dollar of money should result in an increase of $8.20 in M2. That multiplier is around 3 today. It historically should be around 8. (Hoisington & Hunt, 2014) This indicates that the Fed's large-scale asset purchases (LSAP) are not currently producing real, tangible economic effects. Make some loans instead of simply placing the money back with the government. No multiplier there. For good or bad, the entire fractional banking system rides on this and it ain't happening. Reduced money growth is an indication that LSAP is becoming more counterproductive. Bear in mind that this doesn't address the merits of the fractional banking system, it just assumes that is what is wanted and needed, not that it is correct.

The velocity of money

This is the speed at which money turns over. If the money supply expands the growth rate should also, assuming velocity stays the same. Problem we have now is velocity is decreasing- mostly because the money isn't getting into the market. The banks are holding it. Lending for productive purposes is a big factor. Productive purposes means the debt must produce an income stream, the debt gets repaid and re-lent again. That doesn't mean student, auto, and other consumption loans don't count. For that matter, then, neither would anything having to do with war.

Will someone explain to me why Treasury bond yields are plunging in spite of the government... even as the Fed winds down Quantitative Easing?

Why rates are so low, and how long can the government get away with it? How is it that the U.S. can get something for nothing, year after year? Some say long-term interest rates are being kept down by foreigners buying U.S. Treasury bonds. To a certain extent that is, or was, true. Asian central banks have supported the dollar by buying U.S. bonds and keeping rates low. They've done this to recycle trade profits back into the American economy which helps to keep us solvent, whether that is their intent or not. Isn't this like us lending money to foreign entities so they can buy our products? My fear is that they really don't want to do this and are seeking alternatives such as the many direct deals like the one between Russia and China in 2014 regarding the sale of oil and gas. Plus these other countries will evolve toward their own domestic markets over the years. The Asian macroeconomic policy will shift from producing cheap goods for America to promoting more balanced growth at home. You can't really blame them, it's not a bad plan all in all. When that happens our bond rates should move up. The same thing goes for the Oil rich countries of the Middle East.

Inverted yield curve

A situation in which short term bond prices are higher than long term bond prices. The more prices on 10-year and 30-year Treasury bonds rise (some say prices controlled by insiders), the tougher it gets for the economy. That's because when short-term bond prices are higher than long-term bond prices, banks have no incentive to lend and liquidity dries up.

The yield curve is the spread between short-term and long-term interest rates and normally one would expect more interest for staying around longer, not knowing what the future will bring. An inverted yield curve used to predict a recession. Anyone. If you were concerned about the immediate or short term future you would demand higher interest rates for your short term money.

Higher bond prices will choke the economy of even more liquidity as the curve inverts further. Consumerism will grind to a halt. The U.S. economy will hit a wall. Assets that went up will come down fast. Then comes a cash crunch. People panic and rush into safe haven investments. Treasury bonds are still the most trusted instruments in the world; they will be popular and their prices will spike even higher. People will talk about a bubble in bonds. The Fed's problem is they'll do anything to avoid this "deflationary" scenario and the bond market knows it. So by choking the economy, the bond market essentially forces the Fed to pump more artificial liquidity into the economy or face financial reckoning day.

Thanks to huge improvement in technology in the final quarter of the 19th century, prices fell. (Hanlon, 2014) People didn't call it deflation. They called it progress. Falling prices used to be a sign of improved efficiency and expanding wealth. Again, in the 1920s there were advances in production techniques. But prices didn't decline. People wondered then why prices had not fallen. Answer: because the central banks were printing money and issuing too much credit, inflating assets.

Today technology has increased labor efficiency, yet, prices don't fall. Central banks don't want prices to fall. So by printing money the Fed is pushing stock prices, real estate and consumer goods prices higher, when prices should have fallen. One hears the question being asked "why this loose credit by the central banks have not been inflationary?" Well, if, consumer prices are rising, not falling; and stocks, bonds and income-producing real estate has exploded, I guess it has.

Stock prices are partly valued based on a discounted flow of dividend income. If the discount rate you use is artificially low, stock prices are artificially high.

Why would investors buy bonds denominated in a currency that the central bank freely admits it intends to inflate/depreciate?" Heavily indebted companies are flooding the market with stock offerings. In some cases they are issuing risky bonds at attractive rates. We all have short memories regarding default risk. Many investors, thanks to the unwise Fed policy of low rates, have been forced to seek our higher yield regardless of the credit risk.

Calculations

In determining GDP numbers, one of its parts is same store sales. It looks like this could be flawed. As one store might go out of business and another would get some of that business. That would mean a percentage increase in the one but in reality the second store lost 100%, unless the remaining store got all 100% plus some.

My incredulity has surfaced before regarding counting credit, government spending, and consumption in determining GDP.

Any article in any self-respecting paper would address the shear foolishness of the CPI (Consumer Price Index) determination. Entire sub papers have been devoted to the joke called hedonics; and to that can be added the changes in how the index is actually calculated.

Unemployment, regardless of what the government numbers say, doesn't count those who have given up and don't show up in any numbers. It doesn't count those who are underemployed. We now have a country full of college educated burger flippers.

Funny how these calculations always help Washington in some way and never help the average consumer.

If you were a prognosticator, what would you use to tell you what's happening? Sales tax receipts?

Why not? Personal consumption accounts for 70% of the US economy, Sales Receipts are reliable because businesses would not over-report taxes. One problem is that food and medicine are not in it. Jobs, of course, but somehow we would have to begin taking into consideration underemployment and those who have given up trying. No jobs, no growing economy. Credit? Not so clear cut. If people are going into debt they are probably confident about the future. You just have to be careful that government spending and credit are not counted.

A couple of things to know when studying the past: Average people didn't have any savings accounts until the 20th century, though the idea started two hundred years earlier (Hogarth, Anguelov, & Lee, 2004).

Inflation in the 1500s was only 1-2% but lasted for 50-100 years so the cumulative amount was high. Tricky tools like indexation were not available until 100 years ago, although used sparingly in the 1700s. (Ehrenberg, Danziger, & San, 1983)

Goldstone and Fisher Wave Theory

The first wave according to Goldstone and Fisher started with the Black Death, mostly in the 14th Century. There was deflation and population loss. Then when the world recovered in the late 15th century (Goldstone, 1991) prices and population increased causing political instability.

Next came the Thirty Years War (1618-1648) full of population decrease (killing), poverty and deflation, followed by the General Crisis of the 17th century (Benedict & Gutmann, 2005). More deflation and population loss. The turn came around 1760 with inflation and population increase creating political instability. Tough decade for Wars. The American Revolution, French Revolution and the Napoleonic Wars.

Finally came the Industrial Revolution in the mid 1800s. Due this time to innovation instead of disaster, prices remained low and there was stability. There did seem to be a problem with deflation. Fisher went it alone and added the inflationary second part to the last wave- from the 1890s through the "Age of Catastrophe" from 1914-1945. (Fisher, 1996) Certainly we did hear of prosperity during the "Gay Nineties and the "Roaring 20s". The political instability is pretty apparent with two World Wars and a Great Depression.

According to Fisher the things these destabilizing waves have in common are erosion of middle class wages, increase in returns to capital and land, inflation and political disorder.

Whether or not these waves are true or not isn't the point. It shows there are a lot of research writers out there and a lot of opinions. But, thinking positively, you have to break a few eggs to make an omelet. We should be able to do better by studying and learning from the past. Looks like we haven't. Inflation was much lower hundreds of years ago, so in spite the new tricks and tools, we are not improving the situation. Or maybe we are our own worst enemy and inflation is worse because of the tricks we have learned.

This theory goes something like this: "A population upsurge creates market demand pressures that cannot be serviced in the short- or medium-term without raising prices. Why not, you ask! You haven't taken into account the contribution the additional population is contributing. Expanding the food supply probably pushes farmers to more distant and less arable land. Maybe. It may become harder to afford "desirable" housing and buyers may compete for what is available. Again we should ask, why? Society's energy sources of choice may be increasingly drawn from less convenient sources. My readings tell me we do just fine replanting timber, and we have an abundance of coal, and now natural gas. A growing population also increases the pool of labor from which employers draw, which pushes down wages in the absence of rapid economic growth. Again, the additional population does create growth, but it should be equal growth in population with equal production. No net gain. This means that, for laborers, the price of consumption goods begins to outpace their wage gains, creating a real deterioration in workers' incomes. My guess is this is just an excuse for management to stick it to the workers. Nice try but too bad the theory is wrong.

Gross domestic product (GDP)

GDP is the most commonly used measure of economic growth, measuring all goods and services produced here domestically. But GDP is inaccurate - a contrivance of Keynesian economists skewed toward a big-government attitude. It increases when the government spends money, regardless of if it's productive or not. Plus it's based on cost, not price.

The way it is structured, it includes government spending on things like salaries, any kind of "make work", programs with billion dollar cost overruns, stimulus programs and of course, wars. Not to mention it includes consumer consumption. How can consuming something be like making something? Seems like a self-fulfilling prophecy where money I spend gets added to a growth figure, proving money I spend improves growth.

If you are a Keynesian you believe that WWII got us out of the Depression. So that means a big enough stimulus will solve economic problems. All that money spent making guns and tanks to kill people and sending boys off to die is somehow a good deal and would boost the economy. Then you count the money wasted on the war as a part of GDP. What a deal

Marginal Utility

Hormesis is when a small dose of something harmful is beneficial, but a large dose is damaging. It was first discovered, in 1888, by a German pharmacologist called Hugo Schulz. Schulz noticed that the growth of yeast could be stimulated by small doses of poisons. (Bonner, 2014) Alcohol is hormetic. In small doses, it is believed to help prevent heart attacks and strokes. Maybe even more. But drink too much, and you'll get hangovers, liver disease or death. Moderate exercise is healthy, but *too much* can cause serious injuries, a stroke, or a heart attack. Snake venom is the same. "Hair of the dog" so to speak.

In Economics this is called "declining marginal utility." Marginal Utility is the additional benefit (utility) that a consumer derives from buying one additional unit of something. At some point, each unit will become less important to you. That's called the Law of Diminishing Marginal Utility, which says the first unit of consumption of something yields more utility than the second and subsequent units, with a continuing reduction for greater amounts.

Marginal cost and revenue is that cost and revenue for the very next unit. Marginal Revenue has to be greater than the Marginal Cost to make economic sense for a company to produce the item. When would the additional unit start costing you more? You reach a point where you have to add another assembly line or hire another worker, etc. Perhaps on the marketing side you have begun to saturate the market and must lower your prices.

Profit reaches its maximum point where marginal revenue equals marginal cost. If marginal revenue is greater than marginal cost at some level of output, marginal profit is positive and thus a greater quantity can be produced, and if marginal revenue is less than marginal cost, marginal profit is negative and a lesser quantity should be produced.

Does the marginal desirability of money decrease as it is accumulated? Sure. Rich people, after the 2nd or 3rd million, don't need or even want as much. How much is enough?

Analysis of Money Circulation and Its Sustainability

Not only has QE stopped, but supposedly so has the big boost that the US used to get from its trade deficits. We got a boost from trade deficits? "I have a brother", said Robin Hood. I guess I read the current account deficit wrong then. How can you reward someone for not balancing the budget? America's current account deficit (the money spent on foreign goods) was as high as $800 billion. Now it's half of that. With luck it will continue reducing because of our reduced dependence on foreign oil. Why is that not a good thing?

Is it possible that the current account deficit is the economy's great problem? Because there is less domestic production, leading to less employment which means less income to spend (demand) on production, perpetuating the cycle. The Federal Reserve has stepped in with their funny money to create domestic demand.

As manufacturing moves overseas, enriching other nations, the higher paying factory job is replaced by low paying service type jobs. The Easy money created by the printing press of the Fed seems to have trouble creating productive employment.

The Feds printing also increases assets such as real estate and the stock market. This creates artificial imagined wealth to spend. Money through debt, not better jobs. Then the pesky consumer takes the money and spends it on more foreign junk, defeating the purpose and making foreigners rich. Even when businesses keep the money they borrow here in the United States, it goes mostly into mergers, acquisitions and stock buy backs, not new plant and equipment investment.

Look around. Very little of the US workforce is engaged in manufacturing, continuing a downward trend. At the same time US profits and profit margins are better than ever, and have actually improved as manufacturing jobs have been lost. Neat for somebody that you can lose manufacturing jobs but still increase profits and margins. Guess who that somebody wasn't? But who has benefited most from the increase in profits and margins? Well, any of the CEOs who aren't in jail have done well. And shareholders. But not everyone is a shareholder. So it seems to me the wealth that's been created has accrued to a smaller number of people than the wealth created early last century during the time of the Robber Barons. Is accumulation of the wealth in a smaller number of hands a necessary byproduct of an improvement in the overall standard of living? Or maybe it is degenerate capitalism or derivative wealth in which the connivers are rewarded and not the producers.

Credit

Time to spread the blame around a bit. We spend most of our time calling out the governments for their wicked ways, but, let's be fair, Joe the Plumber ain't no prize either. When it comes to expecting your things to increase in value, the average guy or gal is no wallflower. I remember reading about retail credit coming into its own sometime during the depression. Certainly it was around before, and certainly, as mentioned below, if controlled, it might even be a viable vehicle. But, it has really geared up recently. Due to the credit card phenomena, people don't even bother to budget anymore. Just charge it. And when the end of the month comes, just roll it over. Sounds just like the government, doesn't it? Oh well, when in Rome. I have postulated before that maybe when the little guy catches on and plays by the same rules, that's when it's time to bail. There seems to be room for only so many shysters in the room at any one time. As an aside, we don't buy nice things even on credit- just junk. Everything is disposable. What's the expression, live it up now, for tomorrow you may die? If most of us had any mathematical sense perhaps we could set up some kind of buy now, pay later scheme. Like governments, if you have a place for a certain amount of interest to be paid in your budget, and it doesn't exceed your ability to pay, that may be OK.

Much of the gripe is about the attitude. It has nothing to do with need anymore, it is all about the want. Gimme, gimme, gimme.

Banks and other credit card issuers have packaged up all those credit loans and sold them back to Wall Street who then packaged them again, (as "safe" debt) and selling them to the retirement fund managers holding your money.

Forcing people into risky stocks is bad business. Many times people will ask, "how come a conservative person like you continues to go out on a limb? Because we have to do it just to keep up.

Does anyone seriously believe a $600 rebate check is going to stem the tide of my demise?

Elsewhere I have oft times stated the verbiage that politicians and corporate CEOs repeatedly deny a problem exists right up until the morning they go bankrupt. In Russia they say, "Nothing is ever more certain than when it has been officially denied."

Forget bottom-fishing for bargains. Thanks to the Fed creating inflation through a weak dollar, there are no bargains.

Get in the right mood for hunting season. Think of the many fiascoes your government has foisted on you. The war on drugs? The war on AIDS? Probably the handling of Ebola, Ukraine, money printing, the war on terror, the war in Iraq, the war in Afghanistan, "bailouts," foreclosure "forgiveness" programs.

Admittedly central planning (Communism) hasn't seemed to work when tried. As in the Soviet Union. Yet I wonder if they had just not spent all the money on war games and hadn't concentrated on killing people, how things might have worked out?

How do you get around corruption? Call it what you will if you believe that's too strong. Regardless, those in the Treasury give favors to their ex banking buddies, those at the Fed are giving favors to their Wall Street buddies, politicians are looking out for themselves and busy buying elections.

CHAPTER SEVEN - FOREIGN POLICY

Saudi Arabia

Speaking of poor foreign policy, what kind of a friendship is it when Saudi Arabia is deliberately driving down prices, not to benefit us but to drive out the competition from the fracking operations here in the USA? I'll bet some of you actually believe that is free enterprise, capitalism and just a fine marketing ploy for corporations or countries. Granted, the Petro Dollar agreement with the Saudis helped the United States greatly for several decades. But our part of the agreement, to protect them and make them obscenely rich, didn't hurt the Saudis either.

The Saudis definitely aren't our friends. Why did the Saudis cut production in the first place? Because they want higher oil prices! If I were a bit more CEO type I might take delight in watching our Arab oil "friends" grind their teeth, because they're selling oil in dollars. Remember, a promise made isn't always a promise kept.

Goldman Sachs see it a little more from the Saudi side. In late December of 2014 Goldman said the decision not to lower production was a message to the United States Shale oil business that it is not in OPEC's interest to balance the market on its own but that U.S. shale oil production should contribute as well, given its scalability." OPEC made it clear that it would tolerate budgetary pain to maintain market share, so "prices could trade lower until evidence of a pull-back from

U.S. Explorers & Producers" OPEC is telling the U.S. to stop pumping out shale gas. Goldman believes The U.S. will take the hint and slow down production and OPEC will implement moderate production cuts once this slowdown is apparent, according to the analysts. (Carlson, 2014) Global politics seems to be a tough business, huh? I repeat, the money our government saves from purchasing foreign oil and the drop in price for what they do buy can go to support the shale oil and gas business in this country. Do we really want to be at the mercy of our supposed friends in the Middle East. One can imagine what our acknowledged enemies would do to us if given the chance. Why are we not better at this game?

Korea

In 2012 Korea was an economic miracle just like Japan was earlier. Korea did this by moving into high-end industries like steel and cars, appliances and computers. They are also income inequitable, corrupt and power hungry just like us. Most people are greedy bastards. Even the very hard-working and industrious South Koreans and the Japanese before them. History shows that excessive greed and leverage always end badly. Unfortunately it sometimes takes a lifetime or more. Too bad for those who suffer through it.

God did not create this country to be a nation of followers," announced Mitt Romney. "America must lead the world. And you think this kind of statement makes us popular throughout the world?

Really? Holy crap. Even if you believe in a supreme being, do you honestly believe the God of Abraham, Isaac, and Jesus of Nazareth, wasted his wisdom on a pretty, rich boy, Wall Street hustler? How'd that go? Mitt. Go forth and beat up everyone you can. Bill Bonner said "That would make Romney right and God a moron. Or maybe He is just having some fun with Mitt Romney." (Bonner, 2011)

Still, why wouldn't we target certain ethnic backgrounds if that's where the problem is coming from? Remember 911? They weren't Irishmen?

Viet Nam

Lessons can be drawn from the Viet Nam era. As is often the case, questioning everything should not only be allowed but encouraged. It keeps people on the straight and narrow. Unfortunately, as in the French Revolution, those who were once trod upon and are now in the position to do something about it, end up being as bad as their predecessors. Questioning needs to come with reason and maturity. Clearly, there is always a risk of not getting that when you place the management of the uprising in the hands of children (meaning college age students). One of the better services of news services is to question what our leaders are doing (a watchdog, if you will) and keep us informed. Naturally they got carried away with themselves too. Questioning should not be done by either smelly wasted hippies who only want free sex and not to work, or by wanna be Hitlers who think they are above common decency themselves.

We don't feel it right for the Russians to be in Cuba or the Ukraine, yet we are in Japan, 50 years after the war. For what? How do you think the Japanese feel? And the Germans? Plus we stick our nose in virtually everyone else's business.

Does the Quran preach violence?

This may sound like a pro Muslim stance but is merely an attempt to be fair. Most of the negatives against Islam are common knowledge here in a Christian nation, so that side has drawn a bye. Point being that you need to know about other cultures in dealing foreign policy. And be willing to consider all viewpoints.

"Fight in the name of your religion with those who fight against you," (Esposito & Mogahed, 2007) First, it hardly says anything very bad and besides, doesn't Christianity do the same thing? Conversely, is there a negative position on women, and are they anti-gay? Again, isn't Christianity also anti-gay? What about the be-headings, killing innocents and using children as shields and bombs? So, how do we explain it when a women is elected head of a Muslim country? Just like Christian countries, some are good and some need some work. Funny that our "allies", the Saudis have as bad a track record as any.

In the Quran 8:72 it say to honor treaties! A multitude of verses in the Quran counsel peace and reconciliation. Maybe they are right to be against our western secular ways. (Esposito & Mogahed, 2007)

As in all religions, the fighting and aggression is by the young men mostly. This is a group that is still wet behind the ears and leads with its heart, not head. That doesn't forget or excuse the old white men in congress who are self-serving.

The Quran says, "Say to the disbelievers, to you, your beliefs, to me, mine"(109:1-6), (Esposito & Mogahed, 2007) Islam instead "urges its followers to treat such people kindly". Some confusion exists in that war is described as "religious" in the sense that the enemies of the Muslims are described as "enemies of God". Could be an interpretation problem there. However, there is ample evidence in the Quran that regardless of the war itself or the reasons for it, the Quran encourages believers to "fight courageously and steadfastly against uncooperative, defiant, rebellious states, be they Muslim or non-Muslim." Fighting in defense of Islam is "a duty that is to be carried out at all costs", where "God grants security to those Muslims who fight in order to halt or repel aggression". (Esposito & Mogahed, 2007) Big difference between aggression (bound to spread the word) and defense. Still a lot like Christianity.

Due to the nomadic and tribal nature of the Arab world before the Middle Ages (700 AD), it is possible that passive resistance would not have worked in that environment. Things change and circumstances change so that what was written hundreds of years ago may not apply today.

And slay them wherever ye find them, and drive them out of the places whence they drove you out, for persecution is worse than slaughter... and fight them until religion is for Allah." (Quran 2:191) (Esposito & Mogahed, 2007) Well, Yeah! Shouldn't you resist persecution? Not so sure about that Allah thing.

Khaled M. Abou El Fadl, aserts that "There is not a single verse in the Quran that calls for an unmitigated, unqualified, or unreserved obligation to fight the unbelievers" (Morrison, 2015). The Quran balances permission to fight the enemy with a strong mandate for making peace: "If your enemy inclines toward peace, then you too should seek peace and put your trust in God" (Quran 8:61) **But when the forbidden months are past, then fight and slay the Pagans wherever ye find them, and seize them, beleaguer them, and lie in wait for them in every stratagem (of war); but if they repent, and establish regular prayers** and practice regular charity, then open the way for them: for Allah is Oft-forgiving, Most Merciful. (Quran, chapter 9) This is another example of something written a thousand years ago and regarded an existing war and peace contract back then. If one among the Pagans ask thee for asylum, grant it to him, so that he may hear the word of Allah; and then escort him to where he can be secure. (Esposito & Mogahed, 2007)

Allah has given preference to those who strive hard and fight with their wealth and their lives above those who sit at home and do nothing. (Quran, 4:95)

Read St. Crispens' day again if you think the Muslims are the only war mongers. Especially as to the praise showered on the soldier verses those who stayed at home.

Those who believe, fight in the cause of Allah, and those who disbelieve, fight in the cause of Satan. So fight you against the friends of Satan. (Quran, 4:76) Hmmm. Trouble here for misinterpretation as to who Satan is.

Specifically as to the Jews, big question as to who shot John first and when. The tribe of Banu Qurayza (Jewish) was guilty of treachery and disloyalty in the battle of the Ahzab. they asked Muhammad to appoint Sa'd ibn Mua'dh as an arbitrator to decide their fate. Since no specific punishment had been revealed in the Quran about the fate of the Jews, Sa'd ibu Mua'dh announced his verdict in accordance with the Torah. As per the Torah, the punishment in such situations was that all men should be put to death; the women and children should be made slaves and the wealth of the whole nation should be distributed among the conquerors. (Deuteronomy, 20:10-14, Farah-Islam Beliefs and Observances pp 52) Looks like both Muhammad and the Hebrews prophets believed their God had sanctioned battle with the enemies of the Lord. (Esposito & Mogahed, 2007)

Much of the Quran speaks of consequences for the Idolaters. That can't be the Jews, they don't believe in worshiping idols either. There is a lot of talk of painful torment to these disbelievers. But then it goes on to say there are no consequences for those with whom there is a treaty, and who have not shown treachery nor have supported anyone against you. So honor the treaty. Indeed, Allah loves those who abide by the limits. Most verses allude to a four month grace period for the enemy to get its act together, and then the killing begins. But, it usually says, if they repent and establish the prayer, then leave them alone. Indeed, Allah is Ever Forgiving, Most Merciful. That last part is seen a lot. Whether it's true or not remains to be seen. That's also the case as to what really happened with the tribe of Banu Qurayza.

Bear in mind that most, if not all, of the above is only one side's version. Esposito and Mogahed definitely cooked the numbers for their book. (Spencer, 2008). "According to Esposito and Mogahed, the proper term for a Muslim who hates America, wants to impose Sharia law, supports suicide bombing, and opposes equal rights for women but does not 'completely' justify 9/11 is . . moderate." (Spencer)

Do you ever wonder if the terrorists have a good reason? The greatest terror insurgencies come from countries that have a very high percentage of Muslim population and are much poorer. It just seems unfair to them that the western countries are so rich. They don't just hate us because of our freedom and values, they hate us because many work much harder than we do for much less of a standard, and have, more often than not, a corrupt government and economic system that favors the few (even more than the US!). The poor versus the rich - it's the same all over the world. Or do they not work harder and merely lust after others' way of life? Or, is it for religious reasons? Killing women and children doesn't seem to be a good game plan regardless. As far as that goes, killing men isn't the greatest idea either.

Ukraine and Russia

The West, led by the ever trouble making US, played a big part in ousting the democratically elected president of Ukraine in 2014 Then we supported the extremist government there now (Milne, 2014). Doesn't look to me like the Russians started this. Russia, understandably, became even more alarmed than usual at the expansionist attitude of NATO and the EU. Rumor has it that the installed extremists in Kiev were recommending extermination of some Russian speakers. Russians, by the way, are the majority in eastern Ukraine. And our NAZI US politicians who started it are surprised Hard to hate Russians when these jerks are running our country.

Trade Deficits

Do they matter or not?' The size of the trade deficit is an indication that America is importing capital faster than it is forming it. To call this a 'capital surplus' might be clever. But to me it suggests that in the aggregate the economy is, in fact, less competitive and getting more so day by day. Is America in financial trouble or not?' Consider the proportion of US Treasuries in the hands of foreign creditors --

something like $2 trillion, or 50% of the total outstanding. When foreign creditors are lending $2 trillion to the US government, something is wrong. Those funds aren't going to cutting-edge private companies or efficient asset-allocators. Instead, this big chunk of change is going to an inefficient government entity, inevitably allocated to pork and guns and butter. "And when you consider how that $2 trillion indirectly props up the housing market and the economy, enabling the hubris of big-bank mortgage lenders with a too-big-to-fail attitude, and keeping long-term interest rates artificially low in the first place -- what you get is a chain of bankers helping bankers that has artificially pumped up the asset-bubble boom.

How come our balance of payments is a huge deficit when we have a weak dollar?

Production coming into a particular region along with investment leads to employment and leads to rising incomes and a higher standard of living. Remember that the next time you read that a company has shifted their operation to Asia. Plus there is a technology transfer that goes along with it. Don't the Chinese just love that? My guess is that knowledge also travels with this production so people become smarter and more confident (or less so). Lastly, here are ancillary businesses like warehousing that say bye bye also. Conversely, can you blame them when, in the United States, it takes longer, takes more people and costs more? So much for our wonderful productivity. Don't think for a minute that this is a low end phenomena. Just look around at all the Asian Doctors, engineers and scientists. In 2004, China graduated around 500,000 engineers and India 200,000, compared to 70,000 in the United States. (National Academy of Engineers, 2008) And they work cheaper. Pretty soon the bright Asians will realize their home countries is where the action is and go home. It should be worrisome that the technological and scientific advantages of the United States and Europe are falling behind. It may also be important to know that any advantage we think we have in the high end services is decreasing and isn't a very big portion of the economy (GDP) anyway compared to the production of goods. We are losing market share and competitiveness.

To stop their currencies from appreciating versus the dollar, foreign central banks had to print local currency to buy these dollars. They then reinvest these dollars back in the US meaning lots of liquidity. This was like QE before there was QE, said Richard Duncan. So less going out to foreigners and less coming back to us, reducing our liquidity and increased asset prices. The energy boom will not help increase asset prices; it will help decrease them. Isn't that a good thing, to reduce the cost of living for the average person? Much has always been made as prices rise as to the effect of oil prices on so many other items, so wouldn't the reverse be true?

Do asset prices need to increase- the money only goes to the rich anyway? Can the money being created by central banks be considered real assets? Can false liquidity really be a good thing? A great debate should take place over this, as well as whether the rich are currently overpaying for things, or as always, those trinkets will continue to go up, thanks to inflation and scarcity.

The Feds are not going to let a de-leveraging take place. That's because that would decrease asset values and force liquidations, decreasing more assets causing more liquidations (in their view). The opposite view is, that is exactly what needs to happen. Most of the leveraged people are either deadbeats or the rich anyway.

The Fed, in manipulating interest and printing money, messes up the natural workings of the economy. Decisions are mistakenly made due to the cheap money, which create asset bubbles.

As government after government has found out, the urge to debase the currency is irresistible. It bails out all kinds of mistakes and allows that government to go to war and placate the unwashed with welfare checks. Guns and Butter, man.

The counterfeiters always get first use of the fake money before its purchasing power is diminished by the increased supply.

If the correction gets out of control, you can bet the government will create more quantitative easing to cover up the pain. In other words, expect inflation. But when can it no longer be controlled? The deflating of the world's asset bubbles is going to happen sooner or later. Doesn't it? Would a dramatic contraction in global economic activity or a long depression in which debts are worked off and paid down, or in which debtors simply default and their creditors forced to take losses be good for everyone eventually?

The Bank of Japan is investing heavily in buying ETFs, and REITs. A bad omen for us to follow.

Protectionism

Protectionism comes about under the guise of protecting American jobs, American Security and American Assets. We do this, I suppose, because we can't compete on the global economy. Knowing that in politics, as in most endeavors, "what's in it for me" takes precedence over what's good for the economy, the environment or the world in general, one would think that the two political parties would jump on protectionism. It's seems easy sell to the public. That lesson should have been learned back when NAFTA was being jammed down everyone's throat in the mid 1990's. Has that really turned out all that well?

On the dark side, you get tainted toothpaste, lead in Mattel toys and who knows what in milk and pet food. When in doubt, remember that; the tainted strawberries came from Mexico, Walmart forced that shirt manufacturer to move to China, and the Republicans think that replacing American steel with foreign steel is somehow good for America.

In having a protectionist discussion, one of the rules to abide by is that the Chinese are not your enemy, their government, your government, their wealthy people and your wealthy people are.

One must question whether quality has anything to do with who wants your products. In the realm of protectionism would it do any good if you produced something no one wanted?

Yet, exports are a small part of the overall economy. Our foreign trade is around 10% of GDP. China and Germany's foreign trade have been running as high as 35% of their GDP. South Korea is the highest at 50% of GDP. Australia's foreign trade has run at between 20% and 24% of GDP in recent years. (Dent, 2014).When high export countries do well, they accumulate foreign exchange reserves and their currencies rise in value. Unfortunately, that ultimately hurts the very exports that created such reserves and so exports tend to fall again. Sounds like a reasonable cycle to me.

Much debate has circulated around just how much the Smoot Hawley Bill, passed in 1930, that raised tariffs, actually contributed to the Great Depression. (Krist, 2014) The bill was passed in order to protect American jobs. Of course, as with money printing today, the rest of the world jumped on the bandwagon and did the same. Stalemate occurs.

As humans we are prone to pick that part of information or an argument that suits our purpose. Protectionism falls squarely into that realm. Besides blaming the Great Depression solely on protectionism we forget that from 1821 to World War II, with a few exceptions, the American tariffs ranged from 25% to 50%. That was the American industrial revolution so it looks like protectionism worked pretty well for us then. From World War II to 1970, tariffs were lowered to 12% and thereafter cut to 5%. Sleeping well at night because you're the good guys is fine, right up to the point when you wake up hungry because you screwed up. (Bonner, 2006)

At some point in time (lord knows when) virtue used to pay. Today you need to either get back to those principles or get with today's program of greed and corruption.

Most free trade advocates, like religious zealots, are for free trade as a matter of principle, facts be damned.

When you have a positive trade balance you gain from having open access to as many markets as possible. For that to happen you must be producing something others want at a reasonable price and/or in a quality manner. But those day are gone here in America. That may have been true when manufacturing was still a major part of the U.S. economy, when people still saved their money and it got reinvested in newer and better production facilities, and long before people expected to get something for nothing. Now we spend money- on trinkets.

Small companies are the life blood of the United States economy, according to common wisdom. Then why have a weak currency due to inflation which only helps a hand full of larger companies? Small companies do little international trading. Naturally this appeals to large companies as it makes it difficult for new market entrants to compete.

One more reason there are very few benefits from a weak dollar.

Like the CEO that swears all is well right up until the morning he declares bankruptcy, maybe we had better adapt another policy. Rather than take the high ground, we had better get some boats that will float. It wouldn't be the first time countries do what's in their best interest.

I guess you could say free trade benefits; if you mean it allows us as a nation to squander what little money we have on the junk. It's just that nothing lasts forever. It is a slow creeping economic death as we become more and more a second rate country. Sooner or later you have to pay the piper. That is what happens when you spend more than you earn. I'll bet Smoot and Hawley are smiling in their graves.

Politics, especially in an election year, is everything. What's good for the country comes in a distant second behind what's good for politicians.

Where does security fit into this picture? The United Arab Emirates once wanted to buy a British port management company that ran six of our nation's ports. (Mauldin, 2006) Is that a risk to security? As in everything, there are two sides to the story. It does seem to make sense to not allow a foreign power to run our ports, so why do we currently allow the Chinese to do it? Seems to me that might give you the opportunity to contaminate something. Those in favor say all they are doing is moving freight and have nothing to do with security. Security is provided by U.S. Customs and the Coast Guard who hire American union workers.

The other big fuss was over The Chinese National Offshore Oil Company, (CNOOC), wanting to buy Unocal (Lee & Douglass, 2005). Does that mean the Chinese are a big Red Menace, or just really good capitalists? Maybe a big Red Menace, if as naysayers such as the chairman of the house Armed Services Committee squeal that "A successful CNOOC bid would increase China's leverage over U.S. interests in Asia." Do you think he has either a vested interest or a constituency to please? Maybe good capitalists (I believe that's a mutually exclusive term), because Unocal, even though an American Company, has most of its reserves closer to Asian markets. Oil companies, like most companies, are whores. They are not American and will sell to the highest bidder. Sadly, that goes for the people bidding against CNOOC. Chevron, one of the bidders is headquartered in California and could care less about American security or its need for oil.

Just for reference and as stated many times, oil prices are not elastic therefore, doesn't do any good to tax it or allow them to raise prices- only the Arab royalty and our oil companies and our government benefit- not the people. I am both amused and amazed that consuming nations such as the United States have been able to reduce the price of oil so much. Not that I am unhappy about it. It's nice to know that sometimes the scam works in your favor. In the long run, however, there is no question that the transfer of wealth to the oil producing countries of the Middle East has been enormous, and probably a death blow to the United

States over time. We shall see how that plays out against our bountiful natural resources and, God forbid, a better work ethic than those in the Middle East.

Past experience when Japan was buying up numerous assets here in the US says it's no big deal. (Mayer, 2005). Plus in 2004 China invested around 500 million here while we invested 15 billion there. Doesn't seem to be a concern.

It may be, just like that of the Japanese, in that Chinese management skills will rub off on American workers. One of the big advantages the Chinese seem to have, again like the Japanese, is that their top management worked its way up from the production floor. There is a real concern that too many American top managers are from sale and finance and don't really know anything about how to make things. That of course is painfully evident in the Wall Street money shuffle. CNOOC has a solid balance sheet, makes money and has cash. Yep, we sure could learn a thing or two from them. America is becoming complacent, uneducated, slow and bureaucratic. (Mayer, 2005)

Happy medium again, folks. Protectionism's effect on the Great Depression is still a debate worth having as it applies to isolation being good or bad. Trade seems to make countries better off so maybe congress should step back a little in wanting to restrict foreign-ownership on roads, telecommunications, airlines, broadcasting, shipping, technology firms, water facilities, buildings, real estate and even U.S. Treasury securities." (Mauldin, 2006) It's not the ownership of these companies, it's the availability and transfer of technology that might be an issue. Besides, it looks bad when we close ranks while advocating that other countries open up their boarders to us.

There is no question that we have some problems to solve when it comes to our competitiveness as well as our foreign trade policy. But there are always solutions to most problems, albeit sometimes painful. We probably should have the government pursue an "anti-dumping" policy against countries exporting goods to the United States at below cost (Labissoniere & Bowe, 2005). Maybe even a tariff that was passed down to the average person rather than hoarded by government.

Loss of employment affects local communities and that should be taken into account in costing products. The ripple effect from the loss of other subcontracting entities and service industries (consuming sectors such as clothing, groceries, and restaurants as well as raw materials, transportation and other supporting sectors) reliant on those industries being farmed out overseas. All of these costs can be used to justify the protectionism needed in keeping industry here in the United States. (Labissoniere & Bowe, 2005).

That is not to say that local industry is preferred regardless of the efficiency level. Bums are bums and should not be tolerated. If the local help can't or won't cut it, then retrain them, re- indoctrinate them or get someone else and relegate the deadbeat to a lessor lifestyle.

Then there is the question and impact of whether or not the unemployed worker leaves the area or merely finds work with another local employer. The latter would beg wonder as to whether or not he/she is taking a job from someone else.

When companies decide to simply stay in business but move their manufacturing base overseas, all is well if the profit spread is passed around to all concerned. That is not the case here in America. The new found profit goes into the pockets of top management only, exacerbating the wealth gap. It appears there is a double negative effect.

Time and time again it appears that government meddling messes things up. That is not to say that government doesn't have a role to play. I have said many times that left to their own discretion, people with power will do what's good for them, not you. Nevertheless, the government also needs to be tweaked a little. Maybe we should start by hiring people who are qualified. After years of American pressure on China to revalue its currency, the yuan, Congress threatened to impose a 27.5% tariff on all Chinese imports if China didn't revalue its currency. (Tier, 2005) In 2015 they did just that, only in the wrong direction- they weakened the Yuan against the dollar- in order to sell more of their exports. Oops! So, let em!

Logic is a poor tool to use with people who are blinded by their emotions and politics. Otherwise, someone would ask the question, is free trade really free?

William Greider asks "Why is the United States one of the few advanced economies that suffers from perennial trade deficits? Why do new trade agreements, despite official promises, always leave the United States with a deeper deficit hole, with another wave of jobs moving overseas? How do the authorities explain the 30-year stagnation of working-class wages that is peculiar to America? Are we supposed to believe that everyone else is simply more competitive or slyly breaking the rules?" (Greider, 2005)

Mr. Greider sees the possibility that the United States can no longer afford globalization, at least not as it now functions. (Greider, 2005) Part of the problem, he says, is that U.S. companies are generally free - and even encouraged by Washington - to shift production to low-wage locations. The practice works for companies and investors, but not so well for a nation.

A small bright spot. If wages are rising overseas, soon there will be a level playing field --- if we produce quality products.

CHAPTER EIGHT - BUSINESS PRINCIPALS

Hyman Minsky

Minsky observed that "stability leads to instability." Most things government and economic are largely cyclical. Stability makes us complacent and, thinking all's well, we get greedier and greedier, taking more and more gambles. Hence business cycles. He also believed more in narrative than math and models. To model things you need to make assumptions, and critics of mainstream economics argue that as the models and math became more and more complex, the assumptions underpinning them became more and more divorced from reality. The models became an end in themselves (Minsky, 2008). Back to human nature again.

Cycles and incompetent implementation

It isn't as though it hasn't been bad before. There is no question that cycles occur. I was just hoping, like so many people, that we were getting better. When people were downsized a decade ago they supposedly reinvented themselves into high tech. Maybe or maybe not. Now high tech is in trouble again, plus some of those people never recovered and were destroyed- economically and emotionally.

Recessions are part of the business cycle. But you have to remember that they are usually necessary because someone got greedy before and expanded and spent too much. There would be too much of everything in the economy so it had to be squeezed out. The Fed thinks it can stop one by printing money. During the 2007-2012 recession that did not appear to work. Politicians and economists speak of unemployment rising a few percent then coming back down and the stock market doing the same thing- dropping but then recovering. A bit glib of them as they fail to discern the heartache caused over that "short" period especially if it's your job that's lost or your investment that went down the drain.

Capitalism seems to operate with unbelievable highs and horrible lows. Isn't there a better way? It must it be a given that politicians may have had good ideas when they came into politics but have long since allowed their politics to cloud their judgment – they never seem to have the "how" of the equation down pat. Recently, my son came to with some concern regarding the Ebola outbreaks. I really have to thank my wonderful country for upsetting my son, and probably millions of others like him. Thanks also to the New Media. I really don't know who's worse. Anything for a story. Is that the result you are striving for in conducting your fear mongering tactics? In observing not only the fear mongering but our handling of the "crisis" I have to wonder whether we are really that stupid or that corrupt or just incompetent? If it were really serious, how come we haven't placed a travel ban in effect from West Africa, (and the transfer flights also -since I know you are going to jump on how tough that would be). Is there some insidious reason the White House is dragging their (his) feet on this? Up until a few weeks ago, if you had forced me to come down on either side, I would have sided with Obama against the Republicans. Now I'm beginning to wonder a bit about this guy. As of October 2014, all of the fatalities were directly related to wrongful contact with an infected person. Again, you mean to tell me our advanced society (or so I keep hearing) can't do a better job? Naturally at this juncture I have to say I have sympathy for those involved who are sick or have passed away, but that is not the point. As far as I'm concerned you can shut Dallas down as well.

Taxes

One hears a lot about the conspiracy of your government spying on you. No doubt your government is made up of shear manure. Most congressmen are lawyers without any sense of morals, slick willies with big smiles or people with too much money who bought their way in. However, I question whether the US government wants to jerk around a bunch of $50,000 a year nobodies. My understanding is they operate on an incentive basis just like all the other corporate criminals, so when your 100 hours are up they just give up and move on. There is no question that large corporations and the rich individuals are cheating the government faster than the government can cheat the little guy. The typical corporation, in spite of whining like crybabies that the United States has the highest corporate tax rate, generally pays a lower effective rate than the average middle class family. That's because of all the loop-holes. Although what they do is not illegal, it sure is not what was intended and doesn't do our standard of living any good. Read your history. Does moral decay have anything to do with civilization's decline? It's kind of like the banks taking huge risks. If they win they get to keep the obscene profits. If they lose the government bails then out. With the corporations, if they lose money they get all kinds of breaks from the government and then when then make money they can used tax credits from previous years to offset. I suggest you take another look at the practice of allowing corporations to move either their headquarters or some subsidiary offshore in order to avoid paying United States taxes.

Several of the nation's largest and richest companies, paid no federal taxes for at least one of the last three years, and nine have escaped taxes the entire time, says The Citizens for Tax Justice study, using data from federal sources such as securities filings (Klinger, Anderson, & Rojas, 2014)

The companies also got millions of dollars each in tax rebates. That's money returned from the Treasury.

The firms claimed they needed the tax rebates and giveaways to promote investment that in turn would create jobs. The catch, the report found, is their investment in new plants and equipment declined by more than 20 percent in the three-year period.

As a result, other U.S. firms and average taxpayers pay a proportionately higher share of taxes, the lawmakers and the report said. Tax avoidance is ruining America while corporate America realizes obscene profits.

I've heard it said that if all the money were divided equally it would all be back in the same hands in a short period of time. Fine. If it's that easy it wouldn't hurt to do it every once in a while. Would that be the same as CEO wages climbing back to outer space in a short period of time? That was OK, wasn't it? Decrease gap between CEO/top workers and average workers. Restrict to a ratio or tax it and redistribute. Yeah, I know that is a bad word and it never works because the people doing the redistributing don't do it correctly. Restrict to 10-20 times that of the lowest paid employee. Tax real estate transfer profits- short term capital gains- and do it at the settlement table! Progressive tax. Severe penalties against the corporation. Make stock options longer (5 years plus) (like bonuses) and you have to pay it back if it goes back down. Heavy jail time for white collar crime. Take their houses from them and put them on the street. Take 10% fee, then invest in Alt energy and manufacturing and helping the poor (but fix/control the welfare system first!) Work with cities. Go after all bonuses already paid and stop new ones- Franklin Raines, Stanley O'Neil, Richard Fuld, Chuck Printz, all Wall Street and Commercial bankers etc. Don't even go there- I know what a nightmare it would be. At least consider something. Pass a law restricting bonuses and don't pay them until a five year wait. Rates were higher in the 60's and 70's- 70-80% progressive – 60% over 500k, and they didn't leave then! (Tax Foundation, 2013) A few maybe, but they always will, so fix that also by freezing their accounts. Let them go! Others will have the opportunity to take their place. Even if the ones who take their place are not as good, they will be good enough and anything they accomplish will be better than we have now. We have nothing to lose since only the rich are getting anything anyway. The rich have been steadily getting more and more tax breaks over the last 30 years. Everyone has a short memory. They whine that we are increasing the tax rate. That's not true. We are merely returning it to where it was. (Same with the "Temporary Tax cuts-which went mostly to the rich anyway. They were temporary! Make it global so the money doesn't run to another country. Freeze bank accounts. But who handles this? Therein lies the problem. You can thank President Bush and politicians like him for giving obscene profits to corporations and the executives while none is being passed down to the average worker and jobs are being lost. On the other hand, Government does need to cooperate and assist industry. With the understanding and string attached that business helps workers.

What about these companies leaving the United States to avoid taxes? Generally they are still maintaining a headquarters and/or manufacturing base here but 20% ownership by the subsidiary is all that is needed to stick it to Uncle Sam and you and me. Result: US tax avoidance. Invariably there is a lower tax base wherever they are going. All the advantages of living and working in the good old USA but at no cost. What should a government do to prevent this?

There must be some kind of "Tower of London" punishment.

And let's not forget Apple. Because so many people are buying IPhones, Apple is in the news for its efforts to manipulate the system. The thing is, if you believe that it is your duty to avoid (legally) as much tax as you can, then there is nothing I can say to convince you otherwise. Over a five year period Apple files 30 billion dollars into one of their shell companies, with absolutely no employees, that found a loophole so they paid **absolutely no taxes. (Dickinson, 2014) You tell** me, is that the spirit of the law? So when the CEO of Apple says they pay all they are supposed those are just hollow words. Obviously the law needs to be changed. I'm not picking on Apple, those mentioned above do the same thing. Can you even imagine how much money is being lost by the government, while the weasels are feeding at the trough in their McMansions.

Another fantastic trick congress has is tacking sneaky loopholes for the privileged on unrelated legislation that has to be passed.

A note should be mentioned here regarding tax rates in general. There is no way the United States can ever compete with the low rates of someplace like Ireland. As far as I know Ireland has no standing Army to protect itself, let alone assist in the Superpower protection racket that the United States conducts. Who is right or wrong is not the subject for debate. The fact is, they don't help police the world so they don't need as high a tax rate. They still can't operate in the black by the way.

Although a politician is a politician regardless of whether a Democrat or a Republican. Both are worthless and, to harken back to Georgie Bush, evil probably. In a cock fight I would still have to give the Republicans the edge. Their pandering to big business is embarrassing as well as a stated mandate in their platform. They don't even try to hide it. I don't know what to say about the Democrats. Their mandate is better, more for equality; but somehow when the smoke clears they can't help being scumbag also. I guess they just don't know any better.

The United States is no longer a democracy, it's an oligopoly. A recent study by Princeton and Northwestern found that the lobbying special interests groups control everything while the average American citizen has no say in anything- and nobody in Washington cares.

Speaking of taxes, this is a list of the various ways in which citizens of the US are taxed: Accounts Receivable Tax, Building Permit Tax, Capital Gains Tax, CDL license Tax, Cigarette Tax, Corporate Income Tax, Court Fines, Dog License Tax, Federal Income Tax, Federal Unemployment Tax, (FUTA), Fishing License Tax, Food License Tax, Fuel permit tax, Gasoline Tax, Hunting License Tax, Inheritance Tax, Inventory tax, IRS Interest Charges (tax on top of tax), IRS Penalties (tax on top of tax), Liquor Tax, Local Income Tax, Luxury Taxes, Marriage License Tax, Medicare Tax, Property Tax, Real Estate Tax,

Septic Permit, Tax, Service Charge Taxes, Social Security Tax, Road Usage Taxes, Sales Taxes, Recreational Vehicle Tax, Toll Booth Taxes, School Tax, State Income Tax, State Unemployment Tax (SUTA), ,Telephone federal excise tax, Telephone federal universal service fee tax, Telephone federal, state and, local surcharge taxes, Telephone minimum usage surcharge tax, Telephone recurring and non-recurring charges tax, Telephone state and local tax, Toll Bridge Taxes, Toll Tunnel Taxes, Traffic Fines, Trailer Registration Tax, Utility Taxes, Vehicle License Registration Tax, Vehicle Sales Tax, Watercraft Registration Tax, Well Permit Tax, Workers Compensation Tax (Durden, 2014a). And the governments still can't balance a budget! Not one of these taxes existed 100 years ago and our nation was the most prosperous in the world, had absolutely no national debt, had the largest middle class in the world and only one parent had to work to support the family. What happened? Gees, I lost track halfway through that list.

Minimum Wage and Unemployment

With wages falling for companies that have, questionably, outsourced their production in order to remain competitive, corporate profitability has been rising. Would any reasonable person believe these two should go together? For the last 50 years or so, corporate profits as a percentage of U.S. GDP were between 3% and 7%. In 2014 they exceed 11% and have been going straight up since 2000 – around the time of the globalization of labor (Yardini & Johnson, 2015). Ask any CEO or corporate guru or Republican and they will smirk and tell you "more for me, less for you".

Those advocating a higher minimum wage argue there's an obvious option: Share those profits more equitably with employees through higher wages and, thus, reduced profits for the capitalists. Redirecting profits into greater employee pay reduces a company's competitiveness in a globalized world. But it's OK to pay themselves more. That called circuitous logic. Or greed. You choose. How can they say they are competitive yet make more profit? The profit going instead to workers would have nothing to do with competitiveness, just reduce profit. Lifting wages necessarily reduces profit margins or it requires consumer costs to rise so that margins are maintained. Duh! Pundits say, "Margins are relevant because, in a capitalist society (and all the other attempts at a political economy have pretty much sucked in the end), a company with shrinking margins relative to peers is less desirable to investors, so the value of the company falls. Competitors, as a direct result, grow stronger, and a vicious cycle begins in which the weaker company keeps growing ever-weaker and, ultimately, either succumbs to its own bloated cost structure or it's consumed by the stronger player which, of course, would then result in widespread layoffs and a restructuring of the weaker company's costs to match the successful company's model." What a load of self-serving crap!

The point being, should the government step in and do something? Teddy Roosevelt thought so. Left to their own devices, corporations will run rough shod over workers.

Productivity is one of the measures of who is losing their job. Since more work falls on the backs of those left behind and they are forced to worker harder, productivity increases on the books. Therefore, higher productivity can very often mean fewer jobs. A great justification for getting rid of employees if you are a CEO seeking to maximize your own pay and bonus.

"A part of the increase you are seeing in unemployment increases is attributable to temporary layoffs in the auto industry," and these layoffs accounted for, "a significant portion" of the rise in the number of filings. (Crutsinger, 2015) I am sure that the people laid off from the auto industry feel a lot better knowing that! My guess is that when these temps go back to work the pencil pushers will not miss a beat in taking credit for that without any footnotes that they were temporarily laid off. Also gains reported are assisted by making assumptions of people getting work that has no basis in fact. Just government mumbo jumbo. I wonder how much validity the current unemployment figures have.

A recent Financial Times article reinforces what is becoming painfully evident: "Wages have flat-lined in the developed world as workers fail to benefit from the uneven global economic recovery."

The National debt was 7.8 trillion in 2008. In 2016 it was 18.8 Trillion (U.S. Treasury, 2016). What does that tell you about how to run a government? Sometime around the fifth grade they taught me you're not supposed to live beyond your means.

Housing

Housing? It is hard to separate from the overall inflation question. Europe has never had the attitude that all are entitled to own a house. Maybe they should be. Unfortunately, there are those among us who just can't seem to get it together or take care of themselves. So, no home ownership, but some decent ability to survive. Living as a serf on someone else's land did have some drawbacks. That's called being sarcastic. It's all part of the same scenario where a few at the top have it all. Only problem with that is we seem to be heading back either to those times or the late 1800s. Both were crummy times for the average person.

I can tell you one thing. Over the past forty years the incentive to somehow finagle you way into a French Chateau or a place in Newport has all but disappeared for many of the upwardly mobile. The gap is just too wide. Once upon a time one could hope and dream, but at $100,000,000 that ship has sailed. Should the government be involved? Maybe, but it needs a lot of work. It's a great idea on paper.

The housing industry is important. If no building, then no construction jobs, no financing jobs, no real estate jobs, less furnishings jobs etc.

Welfare

There are two sides to every coin. No question managers are mean, arrogant, unfeeling, amoral, unreasonable, greedy, and over paid. However, some workers are also overpaid, lazy, talk too much on the phone, do not deserve huge pensions and the quality of work is poor.

At the same time the welfare system does need to be overhauled.

We just don't see that industrious spirit in America anymore. Is it possible that America has lost its edge? We don't have the hunger or lack of shelter found in other parts of the world. We also have a sort of safety net with our food stamps, section 8 housing and welfare programs. Similar to Europe? Boy, I wish I had the savvy and moxie at manipulating the system as some permanent deadbeats have. There is no question that the system overall is skewed toward the top and the rich but that topic is all over this book. How can we improve the existing system, or change to a better one? There is every reason to believe that with the safety net, we have taken away any incentive to work at many lower end jobs. Or upper end jobs for that matter. It seems to be a close call as to whether or not the many social programs have helped our society or not. Those who say no say we have created a sub culture of people very happy to do nothing and to live off of government handouts. We need incentives (or punishments) that motivate people to do something to earn their government check. For those "on the Dole" they averaged $2000 per month. That's more than our poverty level and more than most seniors receive for the money they contributed over a lifetime. Something wrong there folks.

I can think of two solutions, at least. Instead of handing out an unemployment check and food stamps. Number one, use that money to hire the unemployed to work for municipalities or on infrastructure projects; repairing bridges and tunnels and roads, oh my! Or sweeping streets, caring for lawns, painting buildings or picking up trash- anything! Or number two, same jobs just a different name. Have the unemployed do all of the above before they can collect a check on Friday afternoon. The first would probably be better from a feel good plan. People who work feel better about themselves. For any of those who don't like their tasks, that will be incentive for them to get their butts back to work elsewhere! This is government planning to fix the welfare system; it hasn't yet addressed the inequality. Gee, we might even stop a few bridges from falling down.

The law

How come the only one prosecuted in a recent killing episode by a policeman was the guy who caught it on video. So the system set out to get him. Did I misunderstand something here? Our system is not set up to dispense justice, just to punish. Victims are not compensated, and the system costs billions of dollars.

Is it possible that the prison system pushes to convict people because they are profit motivated?

I'm sure there are very good people in the government trying to do a good job. As the expression goes, it only takes one bad apple to spoil the barrel. Sadly, there are many more than just one in this quagmire, and the ratio gets worse as you get toward the top. It's all too easy to do bad things to people when you don't have to put a face to them and they are just numbers.

Education

How about education? Right up there next to health care, government and drug dealers when it comes to fraud. Like the ex-used car salesmen in the mortgage business, there is a for profit college on every street corner. That should be a warning sign right there.

In 1999, 29 for-profit colleges defaulted within five years. In 2009, 47 defaulted within the same time frame. The University of Phoenix only had 1 percent of its total debt balance repaid in 2014. (Krugman, Dewey, Cheatem & Howe, 2015b)

I see two problems without even trying. First, university education costs too much regardless. If it's online it is even worse because the fees are outrageous for not having an campus or other overhead. Second, the level of education has slipped immensely. That says you need to be careful when applying to colleges. Household names, in addition to Phoenix, such as DeVry University and Kaplan College are not without damaging issues either. (Krugman, Dewey, Cheatem & Howe, 2015b) I don't know about the caliber of education but they sure are expensive. There are government watchdogs and remedies for this chicanery, but don't think the process is not unbelievably complicated or that it works well in any fashion. I wouldn't be too optimistic about fairness or results. The tie in here is, our government does more harm than good through giveaway programs which just encourage some to raise their prices.

CHAPTER NINE - TECHNOLOGY

Have we really improved? Automatic transmissions are now electric; but are they any better? And what about the expense? Sometimes simple is better, not always, but sometimes. What makes it better? It would seem that it should last longer and run smoother. It would really be nice if it were easier and less expensive to repair. That's not going to happen.

Is innovation worth it? Is an IPAD or IPhone really worth anything? For the sake of a few, the vast majority suffer. I am not disputing Schumpeter's explanation of Creative Destruction as a force of Capitalism. I'm just saying, Creative destruction ruins people's lives. Again, is it the best system? No one can relax anymore and enjoy life because innovation is moving so fast. I'm not suggesting we go back to the "good ol' days". Remember, as Woody Allen said, "they had no antibiotics!"

Western governments are pushing for minimum wage increases which those same pundits are insinuating is because the governments think that will solve the problem. Granted it will not; however, I suspect the higher minimum wage issue, whether you favor it or not, has nothing to do with technology replacing workers. I have said many times that although high wages and benefits might induce management to look toward machines, management would do that anyway regardless of what wage was paid. Also, when naysayers ask why shouldn't business owners replace workers with machines", the answer is sooner or later the apes will rise up and kill you because they have no incentive to do anything else. When you get up in the morning in Venezuela in the Barrio with a hut with no windows and a mud floor and no job prospects, why not resort to a life of crime- all they can do is kill you, and your family is dying anyway of malnutrition.

None of this takes away from the fact that we in the United States have a lousy secondary school system and are churning out a criminal element without basic life skills, except for a select few. What little education young people do get in channeled in the wrong direction. We are turning out a lot of history majors, liberal arts majors, and sociologists. And college, like health insurance, here in the United States, is outrageously expensive. Would it be nice if everyone had the opportunity to attend college? Sure. Would they want to or are they qualified to? Not so sure.

Will there be problems with that. Yep. As some of those "college material" individuals enter the trades environment they will push out others who are not as smart. It's a problem yes, but maybe a step forward at least. Then there is the supposition that technology isn't able to replace those jobs such as plumbing, electricity, welding, construction, and automotive mechanics. My guess is if they can make hamburgers they can weld.

Supposedly America's manufacturing companies can't find enough qualified workers. Next thing you know they will say that's why they sent their manufacturing overseas. In 2012 Seco Tools in Troy,

Mich., had 11 job openings, paying up to $90,000 annually. It did the right thing by paying signing bonuses and paying for retraining. Mazak Corporation in Florence, Ky. said recently they couldn't find welders. (LeBeau, 2012). How tough would it be to train some welders for a decent wage? They too are offering signing bonuses. What was so tough about that? OMAX Corporation in Kent, Wash., went one better by offering referral fees to current employees. Nobody questions that some jobs have become more complex. Seems like any of the above three solutions would work just fine. This is one of the rare instances when a relatively cheap dollar has made it more profitable for companies to build and ship products out of the U.S. Plus, don't kid yourself, on occasion we can still do a better job than many other countries.

On the dark side, many companies are working overtime rather than hire more employees. Doesn't that concentrate the money in the hands of less people? Even if it is at an average level. With the unemployment rate (real or otherwise) what it is, and many employed in menial tasks, what's wrong with this picture?

More efficient scheduling means more workers on duty during peak sales times without being overstaffed during lulls. Good for business-bad for workers since cost are going up.

Technology in the form of Computer trading programs is, again, an advantage for the rich, but sometimes the programs can't keep up. Computers couldn't compute the level of panic selling in the market. Supposedly that's what happened with Long-Term Capital Management back in the late 1990s. When interest rates swerved, the computer didn't anticipate it. Incidentally, that was a "mere" $4.6 billion problem and it caused market turmoil for several months. (Lowenstein, 2001) I wonder what might happen if a $400 trillion derivatives markets brows up.

Some politicians believe in the "Malthusian Theory", wherein Malthus believed population growth would outrun the ability of the land to feed it. Therefore, demographic growth was a disadvantage back in his time. The theory was wrong then because a lack of productivity and innovation decreased standards and lots of people died. Ergo, plenty of space and food for those remaining. The increase in productivity created over the last century or so has more than made up for that. I guess the assumption is that the productivity innovation and increases will continue to work its magic. OK, let's concede that advances in productivity have helped, but I wouldn't count Malthus out quite yet.

Downloading a high-definition movie takes about seven seconds in Seoul, Hong Kong, Tokyo, Zurich, Bucharest and Paris, and people pay as little as $30 a month for that connection. In Los Angeles, New York and Washington, downloading the same movie takes 1.4 minutes for people with the fastest Internet available, and they pay $300 a month for the privilege, according to the New America Foundation's Open Technology Institute. (Miller, 2014)The reason for this isn't a lack of technology, it's a lack of competition. We have monopolies here.

CHAPTER TEN - IMMIGRATION

How come we continue to feel the need for immigrants? This immigration issue brings up again the "Demand drives supply issue." You have to grow or die in a capitalistic society. When you arrive on our shores, you should be able to contribute work or something productive in the same amount as the demand you bring. The same argument holds in our dealings with the Chinese (or anyone else, for that matter.) If they are producing something, they should have a corresponding need to go with it—or else we don't know how to play the game very well.

Again, it's the humanitarians against the selfish, only this time- surprise, surprise! It feels like the selfish are in the right. Why should we accept refugees from other countries? There are 5.6 billion people in the world with more poverty than Mexico. 3 billion make less than $2 per day. If we allow even 1 or 2 million into our country, with the thought that we are somehow making a humanitarian difference, we will overwhelm our natural resources, social and physical infrastructure. Not only that, but for every 1 million people we take in, 80 million more are added in these impoverished countries because of high birth rates (World Bank, 2012). So much for adopting "little brown babies" or welcoming in the poor Syrians. That doesn't address whether or not the immigrants are currently aggressive or will become aggressively anti American in the future.

The United States is constantly getting grief about our immigration and boarder policies as it applies to Mexico (and those coming through Mexico). Have you tried to get into the European Union lately?

CHAPTER ELEVEN - COMMENTS

Time after time people think they can beat the system. Way back when, there was Rome, then the mid-western real-estate speculators from the 1830s... the railroad tycoons and speculators of the early 1870s... the stock speculators of 1929... the gold speculators in 1980... the tech-stock traders of early 2000... the real-estate flippers in 2006 and the Wall Street shysters of leverage buyouts, mortgage-backed securities, collateralized debt obligations and credit default swaps of 2007. Preceding those greedy fools was the creation of the Federal Reserve in 1913, new deal legislation in the 1930s, Trade and Budget deficits almost all the time, the removal of the gold standard during the Second World War and under Nixon, and finally George Bush proving either anyone can be president or we don't need one.

Before consumption drove the economy, what did?

Nearly *half* of all American households spend more than they make each year. And 60% don't even have more than three months of savings stored up. (Reeves, 2012)

Banks and other credit card issuers have packaged up all those credit loans and sold them back to Wall Street who then packaged them again, (as "safe" debt) and selling them to the retirement fund managers holding your money.

Forcing people into risky stocks is bad business. Many times people will ask, "how come a conservative person like you continues to go out on a limb? Because we have to do it just to keep up.

Does anyone seriously believe a $600 rebate check is going to do any good?

Forget bottom-fishing for bargains. Thanks to the Fed creating inflation through a weak dollar, there are no bargains.

Get in the right mood for hunting season. Think of the many fiascoes your government has stuck you with. The war on drugs? The war on AIDS? Probably the handling of Ebola, Ukraine, money printing, the war on terror, the war in Iraq, the war in Afghanistan, "bailouts," foreclosure "forgiveness" programs.

How do you get around corruption? Call it what you will if you believe that's too strong. Regardless, those in the Treasury give favors to their ex banking buddies, those at the Fed are giving favors to their Wall Street buddies, politicians are looking out for themselves and busy buying elections.

Don't you just love self-policing? It has worked so well on Wall Street. Even in this "Mark to Model" pricing where a bank gets to set the value of its own assets, using its own formula. Gee, I wish I could do that. No conflict of interest there, huh? By the way, the assets we are talking about are sub-prime collateralized mortgages. Oops.

Today the problems aren't much different than they have been many times in the past. We have way too much debt. In 2008 it was 133% of disposable income (Federal Reserve Board of San Francisco, 2009). Since then it has eased a bit but debt is still way too high. Too many cars, too many houses that are too big. We even eat too much. There are not enough decent jobs, especially for the less fortunate. Any unemployment figures are totally fabricated excluding the underemployed and those who have given up and are simply not in the system. Because of not having work as well as learning to be just like the rich, more people are defaulting on mortgages and credit cards. And did I mention our government is out of control, spending too much and caring only about re-election while hating their worthy opponents. That sword cuts both ways. Did I mention how obscenely expensive education and health care are? Not to mention food and energy. Lump it all together and there is also no tax revenue which only exacerbates the budget deficits at state levels as well as the federal government.

Is Greed & Struggle Necessary for Survival

Most people certainly want to be wealthier. Everyone wants to retire early and live happily ever after and speculation always seems more attractive than hard work and responsible savings strategies. But every debt and speculation bubble in history has been followed by a depression, deflation and a long period of austerity. Don't you think as a responsible government you should know this and act accordingly? Do we need struggle to exist? Or when production reaches a certain point where we have nothing but free time, will we be able to relax, read and learn.

Life does suck, no doubt. In addition to the unfair system that rewards the rich, most of us have plenty of character flaws, such as being mean, lazy and uneducated. Remember, you can't fight city hall so make the best of it. Working hard doesn't guarantee success but it can't hurt. I figure 45% of us are the mean, lazy uneducated kind, 45% are the mean, self-serving kind who would throw their mother under a bus and 10% are worth knowing. Not very good odds. Makes for a lot of work seeking the good guys out.

By the way, train kids as you would a good strong dog- a Chow maybe. A strong willed loyal person/dog should not be treated with harshness. How does this tie in to our propensity to admire meanness and aggressiveness? Does success justify meanness? The difference between this and the war stance above is that the strong dog is not innately evil.

Cypress Semiconductor CEO T.J. Rodgers said once, "The killer factor in California for a manufacturer to create, say, a thousand blue-collar jobs is a hostile government that doesn't want you there and demonstrates it in thousands of ways" (McCullagh, 2010). So much for good government- unless they have figured out a way to exist without heavy industry. Their inability to balance a budget would say otherwise.

We do have a major macro-economic problem. In addition to our extremely poor work attitude, we make too much money compared too much of the rest of the world. The American worker isn't competing effectively with foreign workers. The foreign workers work harder, get less pay and perform higher-quality work. The foreign workers are not constantly complaining. The domestic workers believe they are 'entitled.' While we're working on legit issues, let's deal with "are you or are you not entitled to a home, and at what amount and size and where?" (McCullagh, 2010)

Do you think we over-react? This is a country that, rather than open up new energy sources, would pass laws preventing exploration.

Who is to blame here? Well, everyone is to blame: oil companies, oil producers, speculators, being the reserve currency that allowed the United States to print money without restrictions or repercussions, hedge funds buying futures, Wall Street manipulation and insiders, a weak dollar, greed in general (the self-employed electricians, plumbers, HVAC, labor unions in the auto industry etc.), Government war mongering, pork legislation, lobbyists, the un-level playing field favoring the rich, a litigious attitude and the resultant wealth going to lawyers, bank bailouts, subprime lending, not living within our means, big gas guzzlers, no manufacturing, poor immigration policy—immigrants are taking jobs and getting freebies—food, education, health, politicians (infighting, corruption and stalemate, generous health plans and pensions), and bully policeman. Enough?

Recently, a new phenomenon has risen, that of thinking Governments can control an outcome. Now the government is not allowing nature to do its job and de-leverage. Government is also unwilling to admit that the problem was caused by them in the first place by, wait for it-- creating the debt and bubble in the first place! Remember, deflation happens in order to clean up after the inflation mess. Now their idea is to bail out the very culprits that caused the problem in the first place- the banks.

Tell me again why my government is doing such a great job for me and I should be happy? I see high debt, low wage growth, poor employment prospects and increasing prices. Where again is the silver lining in that?

If you want to know where the "great expansion" of our economy came from, don't bother to look for any new ingenuity or harder work of any kind. We didn't earn it, we borrowed it. But over the long term if credit increases at 7% and wages increase at 3% that's a whoop de do. And although it's been stated that we have a decline in debt of 4.5% since the peak (as of 2010), that is a drop in the bucket and if you believe we rate a pat on the back, cause "problem solved", you're delusional. That bubble took decades to create. While at least a step in the right direction, it's still a joke.

We've spent the decade from 1999 to 2009 without returning one net person on an annualized basis to the labor force – in fact we lost some. Not only that but we also added 25 million more people to the population and none of them are working.

By some accounts debt was 170% of GDP in the 1980s and in 2009 it was 370%. (Dalio, 2015) Liars and figures, you know. Nevertheless, we definitely are increasing out debt load. The money went to handouts for the poor, to bail out Wall Street and the commercial banks, and increase the stock market and other assets to help out the rich.

$1.5 trillion of new debt was required to finance the spending. It was mostly purchased by the Federal Reserve with newly printed money they didn't have to buy the Treasuries.

There are many who argue that we "had to" do all this to avoid an economic collapse. Wake up Keynes, you can't live beyond your budget indefinitely. Better to feel the pain now and start anew. I realize nothing is that simple and in some cases, it would merely be a continuation of the banker bailouts. The undeserving should somehow be excluded- but how? Besides, you can never take back handouts.

What else? Poor health care policy. Inability of our congress to agree on anything. Continuing to ship jobs overseas. Spoiled attitudes about what we think we are entitled to, and the consequent debt we have accumulated both governmentally and privately. And finally, bailouts of bums.

Health care is the largest US industry, comprising 17.2% of the economy in 2012. (Hoisington & Hunt, 2014) That's more than twice as large as residential construction, oil and gas exploration, and the automotive sectors combined. Shouldn't the government be doing something about the high prices? Is Obamacare (the Affordable Care Act-ACA) good for us or bad? Is the additional expense to small businesses critical? Or, does it merely mean the owners will only take home $286,000 instead of $290,000 this year? One thing it does is divert congressional attention (especially Republican) from more important issues. If you spend all your time moaning and gripping about your opponents you have no time for constructive efforts. Although necessary to a certain extent, history seems to indicate government involvement and regulation don't help innovation. The question might be, is the extra innovation worth the misery for the average person?

Is the cut off point for catastrophe and doomsday where the governments' ability to tax no longer covers the interest on the debt? We have known this to be true for hundreds of years. This doesn't even begin to address the Feds' printing of money from nothing.

Would a huge increase in energy prices do us in, or will it be the destruction of the employment base due to off-shoring of jobs or the printing of money that ultimately destroys the funding capacity of the government itself?

Can this continue indefinitely? Not a prayer. So how is the government getting away with it? And what's the plan to exit this mess?

How come people are not more concerned about the deficits? They clearly are not or rates would be much higher to reflect that risk factor. How come people are not concerned about inflation either?

Corporate profits are at record levels. By one calculation (Andrew Smithers of Wall Street Revalued) using the Fed's Flow of Funds report, corporate profit margins were at 36% in the first quarter of 2010. Cap Gemini's latest Wealth Report notes that the North American rich saw an 18% jump in their wealth last year. (Arends, 2010) Yet over fifty million people are on food stamps or welfare. Seriously? Why aren't you rioting in the streets?

We keep hearing about the expenses and how we must curtail them. That's Washington speaking. But the Republicans won't cut defense spending, which as I have stated many times, is around ten times as much as the next ten countries spend altogether. Debt interest would not be an issue if you didn't spend money you didn't have. So, instead, our government wants to take money away from the elderly. As for the rest of the budget, if you believe the numbers, the budget is "only" around 10% of GDP. It is said that it has been 6-9% for decades. Maybe so, in which case it's back to the discussion on inflation pushing up the GDP benchmark allowing the budget increases, and is that OK? By the way, don't we all know that GDP is around $18 trillion and the yearly budget is well over $3 trillion?

Ben Bernanke was, and is, a really smart guy and doesn't seem to be a bad guy- like Hank Paulson etc. Pumping the economy seems good but they did it wrong by bailing out the banks with no restrictions on them to lend or not pay bonuses. Obama also blew this.

Capitalists argue that the pursuit of wealth itself improved the lot of the poor and average. Even assuming that were true, expressions like "spoils and leftovers" come to mind. They point to the rise of industrialists in the late 19th century as evidence of new innovations that helped everybody, such as long-distance railroads, household electricity, and many time- and labor-saving inventions. The big question is always, would it have happened anyway? Even then their greed and excess led to clamp downs such as the institution of the income tax, tougher federal regulation on businesses and the best of all, labor unions.

American democracy today bears no resemblance to anything the forefathers had in mind. Not that human nature then was any better than now, I just don't believe they had lobbyists. I'm sure corruption has been around since the Big Bang, we are just finding new and more intriguing ways to implement it. I don't know that we're any worse, just not any better. Crooks and politicians love technology too. Besides, communication is a lot better since the days of the pony express. The token legislation passed such as Dodd-Frank has little or no teeth and I'm sure the Wall Street cronies are laughing to themselves over it. Yet, Americans elected a black socialist over a capitalist in the last presidential election. Now I'm really confused. Granted, in my opinion, he was the better candidate regardless, but how in the world did this red neck, bigoted bible toting group of misfits ever do that?

Didn't anyone ever tell you that you have a responsibility (Noblesse Oblige) to take care of those less fortunate, the frail, weak and vulnerable?

Thousands of people die every day from hunger, even though food is available, and often wasted.

Planned Obsolescence

Some people might think this next rant humorous. I prefer to believe it is just incredulous. If you want to know why nothing seems to get done right and we constantly stumble from bad idea to bad idea, interspersed with wars; look no further than the coined phrase of "Planned Obsolescence". The Auto Industry is the easiest to recognize. Again, we laugh about it around the dinner table but nevertheless, it is still the norm for business today. American car manufacturers (I can't speak quite so much to other countries) certainly wouldn't dream of building a car that will last for longer than three years. I know that's a bit of an exaggeration but what the heck. If you were in the Automotive business, wouldn't you? You make your money by selling new cars and repairing older ones. What's not to understand? It just brings up the concern again regarding greed. How much is enough? Besides, it reflects badly on a nation's moral fiber and character. That kind of attitude permeates throughout every facet of our being (and eventually leads to decay and ruin). This is easier to follow by addressing certain industry groups such as real estate and insurance. How many times have you tried to contact your agent but can't? They're just swamped. They call that success. I call it poor customer relations. If you can't service your clients you have more clients than you were meant to service properly. So, hire more help (which now places the performance out of your hands and eliminates the reason I came to you in the first place), or simply don't take on any more customers and leave a few for another agent to make a living. I had a real estate agent once tell me in a boastful tone that they had 250 listings. Are you kidding me? I wouldn't want to work with that agent if they had 25 listings! There is only so much you can do and do well. So I guess there are two rants in this paragraph. Ever wonder where all the help went in any large department store?

Another major flaw in capitalism, which should be somehow addressed and controlled by the government is tariffs. When the US government raises tariffs, American Car companies simply raise their prices right along with it to make more profit instead of taking advantage of the spread that is created to capture market share and give the consumer a break.

Washington considers you fit only to vote, fight in wars, and buy stuff you don't need.

Does Capitalism work?

Of course it does. If a business doesn't earn a profit, it goes broke. So, if the automakers don't earn any money, they go out of business, right? Then, a new more lean business starts up to do their job better. Oh wait, that only if the government help you out. So much for Capitalism and the freedom to fail. Back to Crony-Capitalism where it's who you know or who you can bribe; who has the money and lots of regulatory hoops to jump through (which only the rich and connected know how to jump through). Democracies have an evolutionary cycle.

Capital investment and the growth it creates is self-financing; and reinvestment creates recurrent employment without any additions to debt.   In contrast, unproductive government and consumer debt automatically feed on themselves.

First of all, it may be important to realize that what we think of as Capitalism today isn't any such thing. It's Crony capitalism. Capitalism or free trade or freedom to fail just doesn't exist. Capitalism, as opposed to some fictional "clean little game" consists of unrestrained amoral behavior in which the schmucks at the top who completely lack a conscience also get to enjoy the perverse pleasure of causing thousands of people to lose their jobs.

It's like Dickens' London or the Aristocracy in France. Capitalism is a Predatory Market environment. It's also not a Democracy, even though a democracy isn't anything to write home about either. China has capitalism yet communism. So there.

Capitalism is supposed to be good because if you work hard you will be rewarded. Not true - garbage men work hard. Lots of people work hard in inclement weather.

Capitalism and democracy are supposed to correct mistakes quicker. By that I mean at least in four years you can vote out the mistake. Of course, one can do a lot of damage in just four years.

Capitalism and democracy were supposed to be

systems based on merit. The cream would rise to the top. What the heck happened? How come we don't have men (women) like Hamilton, Jay, Jefferson (a scientist, architect, philosopher, and inventor), Adams and Madison around anymore? Or are we wrong about them? Were they just like the current crop?

Creative Destruction or a Friendly Society?

The difference supposedly, between government and business is that business give something in return so it's called "money by persuasion": "give me some of your money, I'll give you a house."

Capitalism is working as it is supposed to: creating as much wealth as humanly possible. Hooray for capitalism. The assumption that it makes everybody's lives better however, is just not true. I am having trouble following. If lives are not any better, then why bother to create all that wealth? Or, as I suspect, is the wealth not being distributed equally? We need to examine the play book again to see exactly what the purpose is for civilization.

Economic historian Deirdre McCloskey doesn't see the Industrial Revolution and beyond happening on the backs of slaves, but by "changes in the way people thought, and especially how they thought about each other." I'd say there was a better chance for the slave argument, even if not entirely correct.

The average person not only doesn't have a clue what the phrase means but certainly does not like any kind of change, especially if that "creative destruction" loses them their job. Creativity does have a way of changing things. But, for the better? That isn't as certain.

In the old days people who merely bought and sold things for a living were scorned as peddler and cheats. Not really well respected. Apparently there is less shame in that now. I often wonder just how bad things really were in the old days on the frontier. Yes, people wore guns and life on the prairie was tough. But were they happy and did they get enough to eat? It's just hard to compare apples to apples, the entire manner of living was different. Are the toys of today's technology necessary? Think the IPhone/Ipad fantasy.

Of course progress has been made. The middle class probably does have more liberty, better access to education ,the ability to travel to farther places, more equality (for some), access to more information and more leisure time. That doesn't mean things are hunky dory.

It does appear that in India and China have done well in adopting liberal economies with a profit motive, but, welcoming creative destruction? Come on! Not likely. Improvements of late, like more democracy, the liberation of women, improved life expectancy, greater education, spiritual growth, and artistic expression are all the result of capitalism (McClosky, 2010). Sheer speculation!

Anti-capitalists insist it has been FDR's New Deal, the Tennessee Valley Authority (TVA) and the Federal Deposit Insurance Corporation (FDIC), to name a few government programs that have created the dandy living we enjoy. (French, 2014) There may or may not be some truth to that. However, while these folks want to blame dog-eat-dog, cowboy capitalism for the crash of 2007-09 (The very fact that they use those terms should make you suspicious of their theories), it was, in fact, directly a result of Roosevelt's creation of depression-era pro-housing government programs like the FHA, Fannie Mae, Freddie Mac, and deposit insurance, that codified moral hazard into banking. (French) No doubt there is some truth in this as well, but it may be unfair to lump them all together. As I explained in the Depression Era section, even though his heart was in the right place, there were flaws in the spending of the New Deal.

Where would the money come from to wander around the planet fighting wars? Pity the poor Republican. It was Obama (not saying I'm a fan) who said capitalism didn't work when it was tried in the 1920s, it's didn't lead to the postwar booms of the '50s and '60s, and it didn't work during the last decade.

I cannot disagree that big government is a culprit as evidenced by the fact that the currency is worth a fraction of what it once was. But can we blame that on capitalism? Maybe.

A great example of the corruptive immorality and injustice of the US government is the recent IRS comedy hour in which seven hard drives crashed at the same time and a simple "sorry" got them out of any responsibility. The expression for what they were doing is "political thuggery." Someone said the odds of 7 drives crashing at once was 1 in 78,664,164,096. (Giles, 2014)Like the bank, sub-prime and economic downturn scandals, the probability of the crook going to jail is still zero. And one more thing: There was someone on the other end of all those emails. Why not get copies from them, or from the mail administrators in-between? Or from whoever in the government is spying on them? They do that don't they?

Even though it may keep prices line, is cheating everyone in every deal worth it? Are we happy in a society where the business model clearly is to cheat each other? We are always negotiating price and browbeating someone. Then we make a TV series out of it starring Donald Trump. Glorifying pushiness and cutthroat attitudes from someone who got the start from his father, lost it several times and merely owed so much they couldn't foreclose on him.

Cowboys and Sheiks

Sure the left is a bit weak and waffling and turn the other cheek, but the Republican side gives way too much credit to the cowboy mentality. Yes, we should protect ourselves, especially if you can't reason with the adversary who doesn't share your beliefs of right and wrong and believes he/she will be rewarded in the afterlife. Most religions have that same belief. Perhaps that says why religion may not be such a good thing. Did the Jews do something wrong initially or are the Arabs inferior and therefore unreasonable as one commentator said. A second commentator said the

Arab Sheiks christened by Churchill were nothing but sheepherders. If you took Israel out of the equation it would not diminish the problems, the Arabs hate each other also. It's no different from trying to reason with some no toothed deliverance type hiding out in the hills of West Virginia. Insisting on me being dead (As the Arabs seem to regarding the Israelis) is not a great platform for negotiation. That commentator also said the Jewish claim to Israel was not historic but economic because they cultivated the land and made it fertile. They are hard-working, but at what costs? Yet there is a reverse discrimination toward the gentile-somewhat like the hatred of the infidel by the Arabs. Man, who's right here? There is certainly some truth in that the only defense against evil is force. If you care for the sick, downtrodden, elderly and weak, as well as love art, poetry and beauty, then you had better be prepared to kill for them. You have to be willing to wipe out the enemy. The West has gone overboard in their belief in not killing civilians so that basically guarantees we can't totally win a war. Whereas, if we did thoroughly win maybe we wouldn't have to go back over and over again. I hate it, but it's a cruel world.

Some people are barbarians and you can't negotiate with someone who wants you dead. Islam condones subjugation of women, killing homosexuals and killing civilians in battle. Even placing your own children in the line of battle so the other side will either not fire on them or will catch public wrath for doing so (King, 2014). If you don't agree that's a flaw, then at least agree there is a fundamental difference. Let's go with there is a problem here. Who's the bad guy? According to the Old Testament the Philistines filled in the Jewish wells with sand when they confiscated them. Or smashing greenhouses they confiscated instead of using them. Smart. To be fair though, let's not leave the conversation without looking at what the Christians and Jews have done.

You can't get along with your spouse, how are you going to get along with someone 10,000 miles away or of a different skin color or religious belief?

What is going on in those Mosques? Are you preaching love and compassion and getting along, or kill whitey and/or the Christian?

Multi-culture environments. Good or bad? Seems like assimilation is the better way to go. You can still retain your own cultural customs but if you came here for opportunity then make an effort to fit in, otherwise, you have these enclave, hot beds of festering hostility against all those who are different. You don't like it- go back home, wherever that is. Government? You have to set the example.

Point being, lots of good and bad on all sides. Study up people!

Sociopaths

There is an entire school of thought that, even though human nature is innately not very nice, there is a sub class that's really nasty! Problem is that these people run the governments! John Mark Mattox said that religious philosopher Saint Augustine was pessimistic of human nature, believing men weren't inclined toward righteousness, but instead had a tendency toward doing evil, the lust for domination, which entice men towards waging wars and committing all manner of violence." (Mattox, 2006) Yep.

Paul Rosenberg comments that "Predators walk among us, they are without a conscience and they are indistinguishable from normal people. These differently wired humans have a predatory advantage, and they use it. These predators are called sociopaths or psychopaths. He says that at least 2% of the overall populace are sociopaths or predators, and some estimates are double that (Rosenburg, 2014). We would like to believe the old religious doctrine that everyone has some good in them. Yeah, right. Start over and read the above again.

Sociopaths don't have much in the way of positive emotions themselves, so they fake them. They don't get embarrassed. But nobody is perfect at faking. They learn to mimic normal behavior and hide their own.

Sociopaths lack empathy for the feelings of others or conscience. They don't feel bad about abusing other people. It's not that they feel bad and ignore it— they don't feel it at all. They have no empathy, no remorse and are users. These are weaknesses.

Sociopaths are excellent liars. Even able to pass lie detector tests. A sociopath will actually work a plan to get a group of people who believe in him or her.

Trying to repair a sociopath is like trying to roll a ball uphill. It just tells him that you're a ripe sucker. He'll play along, tell you what you want to hear, fake the emotions he thinks you'll respond to, and bleed you dry, emotionally and physically. And he'll never feel a moment's remorse as you finally contemplate suicide (Rosenburg, 2014). Think about that the next time you think about sending money to some stock broker con man over the phone or some religious zealot, or the guy wanting to repave your driveway, or your local politician!

Back on track though; human nature being what it is (lousy) with a preponderance of the baddies in the government, what to do, what to do? Governments have, over the last century, killed approximately 260 million people. (Rummel, 1994) Governments, like all hierarchies, are havens for sociopaths. The good news emanating from speedy communications is that it seems people are beginning to realize how really corrupt their government employees are. They are electing incompetents at best, and crooks, at worst (French, 2014). But, the "right people" aren't (and won't be) running for office. Instead, we will continue to have "the average American legislator who is not only an ass," as H.L. Mencken (The Sage of Baltimore) wrote, "but also an oblique, sinister, depraved, and knavish fellow. "No matter who wins, a Sociopath is elected (French). Mencken also wrote, "This election season, remember that it's become "a psychic impossibility for a gentleman to hold office under the Federal Union." It begs the question, "Do bad people become lawyers or do they get bad just by being a lawyer?" It is possible that good people with good intentions enter politics but then realize the system requires conniving to operate. To stay in office you learn to lie, cheat, steal, manipulate, and kill (that what happens when you send young people to fight stupid wars). That doesn't begin to address the bribery and lobbying issue. Machiavellian means. What a great phrase.

Charles Derber in *The Pursuit of Attention: Power and Ego in Everyday Life*, stated that "politicians since Caesar and Napoleon have been driven by overweening egos and an insatiable hunger for public adulation." (Derber, 2000)

Abraham Maslow described his self actualizers as being creative and inventive, having strong ethics, a self-deprecating sense of humor, humility and respect for others, and enjoyment of autonomy and solitude instead of shallow relationships with many people. Huh? No politicians here. However, next step down is the need for esteem and, although there are some good types of esteem seeking such as freedom, independence, confidence, and achievement, the politicians go mostly for the need for the respect of others, the need for status, fame, glory, recognition, attention, reputation, appreciation, dignity, even dominance." (McLoad, 2007) "The negative version of these needs is low self-esteem and inferiority complexes," Dr. C. George Boeree, a Maslow expert, writes.

Most people agree that you get elected to public office in this country through either connections, glad handing/big toothed smiling, or personal wealth. a breeding ground for sociopaths. Good people (self-actualizers would have no interest. In contrast, egomaniacs love it. (Boeree, 2006)

Doug Casey said the "moral rot" in Washington, DC, is because sociopaths are fully in control of major American institutions. Their beliefs and attitudes are entrenched throughout the economic, political, intellectual, and psychological/ spiritual fabric of the US.

Wouldn't it be interesting to determine the percentage of sociopaths in certain industries, like sales in general, or real estate, or lawyers?

When things go wrong on a grand scale, it's not just bad luck. It's because of serious character flaws in one or many – or even all – of the players.

Sociopaths are now in control of major American institutions. By constantly blaring their beliefs and attitudes from the bully pulpit normal people start to believe those beliefs.

Most of us think it is different here and the bad things couldn't happen. Silly us. We are not the exceptional country of our forefathers. People are people; given the opportunity bad things are done.

Think about a TSA worker. They are just normal human beings who like to have the upper hand and abuse. There is no difference between them and the average German who joined the Gestapo. Many of them are just mini-sociopaths.

Bear in mind, due to most people being lazy, absorbed in their own little world and not really up for the battle, it only takes a few of these quacks to control any situation.

They seem perfectly normal. They are the weekend jocks and our beer drinking buddies. But these are the people who will join the Gestapo, or the TSA. Many, harken back to the weekend jock attitude and are happy to be bullies if given the chance. A certain percentage of these guys/gals are even worse. They looooove being the bully, (unfortunately, we stupidly idolize many of their qualities) and the government is a fertile stomping ground for them. It welcomes them and they run to it. It gets worse. These people because of their very attitudes and trickiness, rise into positions of leadership. More's the worse for the rest of us. It is a sad fact of life that we hire in our image and remake organizations in that image. Good people, if ever there were any in government, will not like the atmosphere and will leave. Pretty soon there are nothing but sociopaths left.

Because of fools like George Bush, we spend all of our time looking out at the supposedly bad guys like North Korea and Iran. Firstly, they are mostly irrelevant and of no threat, which is probably why we chose to use them. We know better than to mess with China, we may get our clocks cleaned. True, they are, or may be bad guys, but we all miss the point in that the really evil people are right under your nose. Actually Bush is one of the problems, just not as smart as the really bad ones.

You would have to be a sociopath, especially in the Military Industrial Complex, to want to annihilate millions of people just to sell a few weapons and play soldier. Maybe back a few hundred years when war was less dangerous, more controlled and a bit more gentlemanly (although I find that to be a mutually exclusive phrase), it made more sense. But today you are really playing with fire with all the powerful weapons, especially nuclear weapons.

As mentioned many times, asking "how could they do that?" is really shortsighted. You can't possibly know how or why because you are not a sociopath. They are amoral, have no regrets or remorse and simply don't care what happens to others. The cleaver ones are awfully good at pretending otherwise though. As I mentioned above, they are chronic, liars, generally believe their own lies, and are not easy to spot because normal people tend toward assuming you are telling the truth. They blend in and always say the right thing in public. That throws normal people off because they judge by their own decent standards and can't imagine how a congressman who espouses his or her support for good causes could possibly be a bad guy? Sociopaths consider themselves superior to everyone else and they're arrogant. They are never wrong- in their eyes, so they never take responsibility for things going wrong. Bad news is good news to these people. They love to deal in rumors, usually starting them themselves. It would be difficult to emphasize just how dangerous and diabolical these people are.

Again, a governmental organization is such a wonderful playground for these predators, who love to play cops and robbers. They get to wear both hats at once. They get paid to be monsters.

Part of this evolution is our own fault. As mentioned above, we are not perfect and have our own faults. We don't care enough or pay attention. Life is tough and we want to watch some reality TV. Yes, because the lower classes have nothing and are not even in the game they don't care. The upper class is greedy and arrogant- they have it all and actually believe they deserve it. Remember, some inherited it, some got lucky, some are just mean and aggressive nasty humans, and the only the remainder worked hard and smart. That's a fertile field for spin doctors to produce sound bites that the rest of us want to hear. They spend lots of money on surveys to find out exactly what we want to hear.

Digressing for a moment, think of these examples: Mitt Romney is a spoiled little rich boy. He has no clue about the average person, Nancy Pelosi just scares me and John Boehner wouldn't know the truth if it came up and slapped him. I finally figured out what's wrong with John McCain. He is hostile, perhaps because of unpleasantness in his background. That's not a good trait for someone in charge.

A good example of Sociopaths would have been Germany during World War II. Clearly those at the top were sociopaths. What happened? Perfectly normal, decent cultured people followed them. In Germany, don't follow and you die, plus no matter how bad your leaders were, you were led to believe, justifiably so in most cases, that invading armies were coming to rape your daughters, steal your property and probably kill you. I realize that's exactly what your leaders did, but somehow no one caught the similarities. Don't think for a minute that under the same circumstances, every one of us here in America wouldn't do the same thing. Have you really read some of the slogans the Military has? Or your local church for that matter. Throw in a little adversity such as that during the war and watch your neighbors turn on you. Don't follow the sociopaths and the result is death.

History says we did it before, we will do it again. Remember Georgie Bush saying, "If you're not with us, you're against us." What a total ass.

Front Running on Insider Information

How many time must we mention the tremendous perks that our politicians have? From insider information to free and better health care, a phenomenal pension plan and undeserved idol status.

Capitalism versus Communism.

What producers can produce or what consumers want would seems to be a better system than central planning dictating arbitrarily. And yet... The Europeans appear to do this better. Germans determine what will be needed five years from now and train people for it. Universities, governments, and corporations work more closely together. Isn't that central planning of a sort?

How come communism doesn't work? It sure seems like the better system.

Marx versus Schumpeter.

Josef Schumpeter is our boy wearing the white capitalism colors. Industrial gain comes mainly from successful introduction of new products, new forms of production or an improved and more efficient organization. Although generally known for his "Creative destruction" theory, he did say that there was a long term tendency for profits to vanish under capitalism. He also believed that the talk of savings being negative. He was a bit negative on monopoly theory also, because it was narrowly applied and the theory assumes that the demand and costs conditions are the same for competition and monopoly- which they are not in his view. And there are other things besides labor, like capital, material and machinery. (Schumpeter, 1942)

He took an equally pragmatic view of communism, distinguishing between Marxism and other practices such as under the Soviets.

Wearing the dark trunks of communism is Karl Marx. Marx said the capitalists started out great as they eliminated the feudal systems and the religious fervor. Initially a good work ethic was important. They accepted women's rights and believed in no class distinction. Unfortunately it somehow led to the belief that money was the most important thing in life.

Marx- saw society as two classes- the owners and the workers (sellers of their labor-the Proletariat). He felt the system was antagonistic. Capitalists (owners) destroy each other and eventually the system breaks down. He called it primitive accumulation. His was the Labor Theory of Value- that the value of an object is decided by the resources that went into making it. The cost can be composed of any of the factors of production including labor, capital, land, or technology. This as opposed to the Theory of Marginal Utility which includes monopolies, imperfect competition and other factors. To have value an object must be both useful and scarce to a consumer. (Marx, 1867)

Marx was complimentary of capitalism for its ability to create, e.g., the Roman Aqueducts, Egyptian pyramids, and Gothic cathedrals. He was broadminded and respected other (civilizations) etc. Marx extols the power of capitalism to develop capacity to produce-while creating growing misery for the masses. (Marx, 1867)

Marx rejected the "Nursery Tale" that superior intellect and energy and saving resulted in ownership and wealth. His idea was that you got it by force-robbing and subjugating workers- it arose from feudalism which became capitalism. (Marx, 1867)Son of a gun. Been there, done that.

In his Communist Manifesto he alludes to capitalism as needing to be ever expanding. In it, the

Bourgeoisie cannot exist without constantly revolutionizing instruments of productivity and relations of production. That keeps the producers off guard and constantly relearning, never becoming proficient. It is naked, shameless, direct, brutal exploitation. Every expansion leads to imperialism, the last, necessary stage of capitalism. If he is even remotely correct, why would anyone use the system or believe it to be the best way? It also consists of egotistical calculation and enlightened religious fervor. Capitalism converts every honored profession (doctors, lawyers, priests, scientists) into paid wage earners and reduces the family from sentimental concern to mere money. Under Communism, mechanization is improved by reinvestment of surplus capital into plant and equipment, instead of into the pockets of the owners (Marx, 1867)

In one sense Marxism is religion; it has a plan of salvation, standards to judge by and evil to combat. It promises paradise on this side of the grave. Marx was part prophet and part scientist. Although he was a coffeehouse conspirator at times as needed, he despised being that. He basically practiced scientific socialism. Marx was smarter and more learned than most prophets. Clearly, he was more than a purveyor of phraseology or he would not have lasted. He believed, as does any religion, that the enemy is not merely in error but in sin. (Marx, 1867). Sad. Disagree with me and you are not only wrong but intellectually but morally. Marx wasn't vain but he was petty, spiteful and vulgar sometimes.

Marx could spin a tale. He knew to create the feeling of being thwarted and ill-treated. Most people loved the message even though they didn't understand it. Marx really didn't glorify the workman. Even feeling this way he hid the true nature of the workingman which was merely to get ahead a little and have some help getting there. Marx felt the worker acted based on circumstances, not on their own good sense. He looked to a greater social system in spite of the workers. (Marx, 1867)

Without improving on human nature it does seem that centralization of power has a few kinks to work out. He also got carried away a bit, advocating abolishing the right of inheritance, heavy income tax, and no personal property. But, some of the indisputable positives surrounding Marx are: Communism does not discriminate, regardless of nationality. And eliminating nations and religion probably would eliminate a lot of wars.

Unfortunately, you need a revolution to implement most of his ideas. He failed in his prediction of increasing misery--- so far.

Economies require pain

Without the pain of recession one cannot get rid of inefficient industries and clear the way for better, healthier industries or companies. They cannot kick out the old, lame enterprises, for example, or enable the "younger, hotter" enterprises. There you go again, spoiling a true premise with bigoted nonsense. No wonder the elderly are curmudgeons. The elderly have experienced a late life realization that we are a nation, and perhaps world, of youth oriented, throw it away (it being you) culture that considers them a necessary nuisance at best. This, my dears, as Fagin would say, is Schumpeter's "Creative Destruction".

There are many reasons for companies not hiring, some even semi-legitimate like uncertainty over tax policies and the economy in general. Please don't think that the businesses are not giggling about this, or suffering in any way as they fatten up their wallets. All you have to do is look at corporate profits.

Dan Amoss, a newsletter writer, said in 2010 that earnings estimates will have to come back down. He went on to say that he was amazed at how many sell-side analysts were modeling V-shaped recoveries in 2010 earnings. Most stock prices were disconnected from reality (Amoss, 2009) Only the last part proved to be true. Amoss was wrong and the analysts were right, although in my opinion, he was wrong for all the right reasons.

Amoss went on to say "The economically illiterate, and those in favor of big government, will use any crisis as an excuse to expand government. Many in the media and academia clearly do not realize that the government has no resources. It'll take money out of one of your pockets, skim some off for its cronies, and expect you to be grateful when they put some of it -- debased by the Fed's inflation, of course -- back into your other pocket" (Amoss, 2009). He was correct here but the thing to take away from these comments is that there are two sides to every story and everyone has an opinion. Some right, some wrong. Even the love of a good dog has its dark side, and they are much more positive, loving and trustworthy than humans. That doesn't mean I enjoy listening to one yapping from 2 blocks away. See? I guess you learn to take the bad with the good. You just have to learn to take everything with a grain of salt. Based on the situation, Amoss should have been right.

Natural Resources

Governments don't have to try as hard if they have a natural advantage. It is a possibility that is exactly why the United States had such a nice run early in our existence. When we arrived in America there was an abundance of wildlife and natural resources, such as trees, water and plenty of land to grow crops. The weather was reasonable mild. Later we discovered oil and the race was on. The same thing could be said for the Middle East today. In fact, one could say there is far too much wealth in the Middle East. On the other hand, Lord knows what the British had during their day in the Sun. Life just isn't fair. The English/ Spanish/Dutch/ Portuguese, all cheated their way to the top by trading junk for value. The bully tendencies didn't hurt either.

Social Security is great.

Security for the elderly. One of the greatest ideas in the world. What could possibly be wrong with that? Especially when it is mostly or all of their own money? What kind of selfish, self-serving scumbag would be against that? Someone has been watching too much Mad Men (and I don't even know what it's about.) Let's face it, based on human nature not being as good as it could be, concede that most people can't or won't save even to care for themselves. Living in the moment is just too easy. But, as others (the American Indians, the Chinese etc) believe, at 65 you aren't expected to be a contributor anymore. You did your part for 40 years and now have earned the right to enjoy your golden years. In the past I have discussed exactly what the function of government should be. It seems like caring for the elderly might make that list.

Consumers are not spending and that is supposed to be critical. So what? Besides planting and harvesting crops, some Sumerians hunted, fished, or raised livestock. In addition to an increase in population, civilization was also about variety, and enough food was produced to support people who worked at other occupations – such as the priesthood, pottery making, weaving, carpentry and smithing. There were also traders, and the Sumerians developed an extensive commerce by land and sea. They built seaworthy ships, and they imported from afar items made from wood, stone, tin and copper. If they could do it, why can't we? Why then, is it necessary to expand?

Pete Peterson in his "Running On Empty", points to studies done on the future obligations of the Social Security and Medicare trust fund. In 2003, the American Enterprise Institute projected a $45 trillion shortfall; $47 trillion countered the International Monetary Fund in 2004; the National Center for Policy Analysis and the Brookings Institution came up with $50 trillion and $60 trillion respectively in their own research reports published in 2003. In 2004 the Social Security and Medicare trustees themselves estimated the unfunded benefit liabilities to have a current value of $74 trillion dollars. (Peterson, 2004) It wo0uld be nice if they could all agree. Generally, the problem with most of these studies is calling something current that isn't. Current mean now which should mean within a year, and there is no way that's true. They may be meaning that today's estimate of the entire future liabilities would be those figures. That, as stated elsewhere, assuming no income to offset the figures and the fact that the government took what was already in there.

Politicians and the rich spend a lot of time complaining about the "giveaway programs" such as minimum wage, social security, welfare, etc. I guess it's easy to complain about pennies when they make and/or steal millions of dollars. How can you, in all good conscience, be so one sided? If the upper class made a little less maybe we wouldn't have to have these programs. One example of such ridiculousness is Senator Alan Simpson from Wyoming who called senior citizens the Greediest Generation as he compared "Social Security" to a Milk Cow with 310 million teats. This seems so patently ridiculous that I worry about my fellow man if he falls for the logic. As for Simpson, I don't worry about him since he is beyond help. Unfortunately, we are not to the point of simply shooting him, which is what needs to happen. Following is a response to Senator Simpson far better than I could come up with. I want her on my speech writing team. It a letter from a woman in Montana named Patty Myers:

"Hey Alan, let's get a few things straight!

1. As a career politician, you have been on the public dole (teat) for FIFTY YEARS.

2. My Social Security payments, and those of millions of other Americans, were safely tucked away in an interest bearing account for decades until you political pukes decided to raid the account and give OUR money to a bunch of zero losers in return for votes, thus bankrupting the system and turning Social Security into a Ponzi scheme that would make Bernie Madoff proud.

3. Recently, you moved the goalposts for full retirement from age 65 to age 67. NOW, you and your "shill commission" are proposing to move the goalposts YET AGAIN.

4. I, and millions of other Americans, have been paying into Medicare from Day One, and now "you morons" propose to change the rules of the game. Why? Because "you idiots" mismanaged other parts of the economy to such an extent that you need to steal our money from Medicare to pay the bills.

5. I, and millions of other Americans, have been paying income taxes our entire lives, and now you propose to increase our taxes yet again. Why? Because you "incompetents" spent our money and kept right on spending even after you ran out of money. Now, you come to the American taxpayers and say you need more to pay off YOUR debt.

1. How much are you receiving in annual retirement benefits from the American taxpayers?

2. How much do you pay for your government provided health insurance?

3. What cuts in YOUR retirement and health care benefits are you proposing in your disgusting deficit reduction proposal, or as usual, have you exempted yourself and your political cronies?

It is you, Captain Bullshit, and your political co-conspirators called Congress who are the "greedy" ones. It is you and your fellow nutcase thieves who have bankrupted America and stolen the American dream from millions of taxpayers for the sole purpose of advancing your pathetic, political careers.

P.S. Stop calling Social Security benefits "entitlements". WHAT AN INSULT! I have been paying into the SS system for 45 years It's my money - give it back to me the way the system was designed and stop patting yourself on the back like you are being generous by doling out these monthly checks. (Grim, 2010)

Why would people with so much money and power begrudge others a pittance? Social Security is one of those bewildering examples. The Republicans have been trying to kill this program for years. Is it because it is popular and, in spite of everything the rich say, working pretty well. What's not to like that provide a small morsel for the elderly to help in their golden years? Or is it just because these people have no clue what's happening in the lower ranks? The rich do lead such sheltered lives that they really wonder, "Have they no cake?" The wealthy and powerful don't seem to realize that many people on social security work manual labor jobs so their life expectancy hasn't gone up. Plus their salaries haven't gone up and there is no longer a pension plan in place for them. Stephen Moore, a right wing activist, calls it "the soft underbelly of the welfare state" Can't you just picture some speech writer coming up with this pablum? (Krugman, 2015c)

During Bush's tenure he wanted to privatize Social Security. I believe if the average person had been capable of handling their own finances we would have done that way back before Social security was enacted. It's a security blanket and therefore should not be gambled with. Unfortunately many of us are gamblers and need a little help and guidance.

I suspect that raising the retirement age another year is like stepping over a dollar to pick up a dime. Come on guys, you can do better than that. Jeb Bush (no matter how hard I try, I can't stop seeing his brother in him) says that "the retirement age should be pushed back to 68 or 70. Scott Walker agrees. Marco Rubio wants both to raise the retirement age and to cut benefits for higher-income seniors. Even Rand Paul wants to raise the retirement age to 70 and means-test benefits. That should be fun to administer. Ted Cruz wants to revive the Bush privatization plan." (Krugman, 2015c) That should be reason enough to vote Democrat. You would think that since Americans love social security the Republicans would at least pretend to want to help.

The question to ponder is why do the rich hate Social Security so much? They don't even pay into it to the full extent of their earnings, there's a cap on social security.

This is our fault

Whoever us is. I know it's not easy because these guys have all the cards, but gee guys, we should do something. In the past, at least, after a while, the peasants would rise up and revolt, a war broke out or someone got their head chopped off. So be it. You have heard all of the dull platitudes. Someone has to watch the store. Like letting a fox guard the hen house. Given the opportunity we all do bad things and human nature is basically selfish and self-preserving. Self-policing? See the Fox in the Hen house comment above. It has worked so well on Wall Street. Especially with this "Mark to Market" pricing where a bank gets to set the value of its own assets, using its own formula. Gee, I wish I could do that. No conflict of interest there, huh? By the way, the assets we are talking about are sub-prime collateralized mortgages. Oops.

You have got to be diligent and vigilant. Give them an inch and they will take a mile. Some of us still believe just because the rich dribble out a pittance just to keep us in line, they will continue to care for us on some reasonable basis. What baloney. These guys would kill their mothers for a nickel. We are so busy watching reality TV and texting on our IPhones we hardly notice the deterioration.

It makes sense that to be able to cure any ills one should be focused and have an idea of what the problems are. With that in mind, here are a few things we could work on: household net worth is down (people need a cushion, household debt is up (because they have no job or costs are high), the real unemployment rate is very high because people have given up and stopped looking, now the average as well as the rich are delinquent and defaulting on loans, we have little heavy industry (think about the consequences of another conventional war), Banks are greedy, not lending and out of control, Health-care is obscenely expensive, the government is spending money they don't have, and it's going to insiders, we need to resolve the energy-oil crisis, politics is too mean and they can't get anything done, we don't work hard like the Chinese and Indians, our moral values are declining, we have an overextended military industrial complex with a bad attitude, we are riddled with bad, ineffective and too many regulations, and we practice crony capitalism. Wow! That should keep us busy.

For all their supposed intellect and knowledge, the Fed keeps doing things to harm the average person.

St. Louis, President, James Bullard, insisted that Quantitative Easing had worked, because: real interest rates declined, Inflation expectations rose, the dollar depreciated, and equity prices rose. (Bullard, 2010) Let's see, with low rates there is nowhere to go for a decent yield so average people must gamble in the market, a depreciated dollar means the average person must pay more for oil and anything else both domestically and from imports (which we do more than export), assets like real estate and stocks are mostly owned by the rich, and finally, these guys don't seem to be aware they are playing with fire with this inflation thing. How should one feel when your government would gladly destroy your life savings for some theory that says inflation is better than deflation at any cost, and the results mostly favor the rich and powerful. The Feds are in a bind. They can't stop printing or we will be in a recession, especially as to housing, plus they will have to pay more in interest if they raise rates.

For emphasis, I again ask, how long can you perpetrate a hoax? What scares me is, when it comes to inflation, governments have been doing it for thousands of years. I hate to think there is any merit to it other than that beneficial to the government, e.g. paying off their debts cheaply and improving their trade possibilities.

The only reason we don't see the soup lines today is we have unemployment checks, welfare, and food stamps. One in seven Americans receives food stamps. As of 2012, if you calculate unemployment using the pre-1990 methodology, before we used hedonic adjustments to calculating employment, unemployment was 23%! (Williams, 2013)

It's common knowledge that we owe far more now than we did before the debacle of 2005-7. As of 2014 it appears we have learned absolutely nothing from the recent rough times. Real estate is back up in certain markets, the stock market is up, an artificial unemployment rate is down and the average consumer is going into debt again. What's not to like? It does appear that the rubber band is being stretched tighter and tighter to cover over our problems with a thin veneer, thanks to taking on more debt and both husband and wife working. One would think the same credit requirements would apply to governments as they do to mortgage applicants. You should be able to pay off the debt with the income you have now.

Truly part of this problem is that these words, such as inflation, deflation etc, are just words to politicians, economists and CEOs. Many of them don't have a clue and have never seen entire families homeless and with nothing to eat. Why is it that most of the Fed efforts tend to take from the poor and give to the rich? And when do they finally realize it?

Take a look at what the United States has become, and then ask yourself if you have any reason to be concerned. We start with a philosophy that condones and encourages unsustainable debt. Easily we move to the corrupt American legal system that lets the rich go free and unfairly seizes assets and keeps them, to the system itself that does not give any chance to the citizens to determine policy. We have a foreign policy glorifying military aggression and occupation that makes money for large multinationals, while we waste the lives of our soldiers. We think and act like any other Empire- not a good thing. Our militarized police forces are corrupt, out of control and basically unpleasant and unprofessional. Recently the government of Canada warned Canadians to limit the amount of cash they take to the States. We have drug laws that are out of touch with today's society. All this is caused by the rich manipulating elite, special interest groups and the structure of our government system, which rewards glib tongued glad handers. Instead of bloated, mean, lazy, bureaucrats, there are friendly and helpful government employees in other countries, and, in spite of the propaganda to the contrary, over 30 countries, many with government health insurance, have cheaper and better health insurance programs than we do. Our news coverage and even out take on history is right out of George Orwell. Pure crowd control and propaganda supporting those in power.

China is definitely dumping dollars whenever possible, and certainly wants our reign as reserve currency to end. As does Russia (Durden, 2013). Those are two worthy foes, economically and even militarily. Mark my words,, after those two make their deals with each other, they will then start on other Asian countries, the Middle East, South America and Africa. Come to think of it, just who is on our side.

It is difficult to get a handle on government actions and what is right and wrong.. General Motors announced plans to lay off 25,000 people over the next few years. (Isidore, 2005) Remember them, the auto makers that got the bailout? Again, the little worker-bees are paying for the gross stupidity and mismanagement by the executives at GM, all of whom are obviously making more than they are worth. Speaking of feeding at the trough. You have to give the auto industry credit for tenacity. Even as the ink was drying on the admonishment for flying private jets to beggars' meetings, they were back for another bite of the apple. They learned well from their pals on Capital Hill. The final bailout always seems to be more than originally requested. Much like any government cost estimate.

Should the government be concerned if its citizens are hurting? The people are maxed out on their credit cards. The question is, who is to blame? The poor, because they can't handle money and want more than they can have? Or the government and the rich because the system is so one sided that the poor have no choice.

Greece – the worst of the worst

A classic lesson as to why governments don't seem to have it together. Or do they?

I guess Greece figures if they simply stop paying their debt, then everything will be fine. I always wonder if the plan to renege was premeditated. My Econ 101 never explained that.

Did you ever hear of the Mediterranean Diet? Well, welcome to the Mediterranean System of Economics. The Greeks are constantly vying with Argentina to see who can work less and get more for it. Both renege on their word regarding borrowing more often than some of us brush our teeth. (Goldberg, 2015)

The left wingers won the recent election. Why not, they promised the people they could continue sticking it to other Europeans stupid enough to lend them money. One of the first announcements was that that the five years of "humiliation and suffering" inflicted upon Greece by its creditors were over. Huh? I never heard that when they were taking the money in the first place. It's always someone else's fault. These people tell you right to your face that their mandate is to "radically" alter the terms of the bailouts from the suckers that saved them. You gotta give the shysters credit, they sure can work the system. They used the richer, harder working countries in the Euro-zone like toilet paper to satisfy their continued quest for laziness. This is essentially a third world country allowed to borrow at First World German rates, (Lewis, 2011) and our old buddy Goldman Sachs helped them hide much of that debt.

The Greek people are just as corrupt and fraudulent as their government. What would you do if you were the "government"? They want the bailout renegotiated because they think it's not fair. But they agreed! If I were a German and were going to lend you money, wouldn't I have a right to expect you to create an austere environment and use the money wisely? The Greeks didn't do that. Reminds me of the whining about the Great depression and the austerity imposed. All that was being done was wringing out the excess of the previous decade. Wanna play, you gotta pay!

There is some hope that finally those in the Euro-zone have come to realize that Greece doesn't matter. If you want to join a club you have to play by the club rules. I guess there really are nationalistic traits, and the Greeks are fiscally and morally corrupt.

Ironically, the Greeks, like most people in the wrong, probably think they're right. So let them have a temper-tantrum and quit the euro zone. In spite of the United States getting away with it so far, getting out and going back to the Drachma would be problematic for Greece. The game plan would probably involve hyperinflation. The Greek drachma would be so cheap relative to hard currencies that the Greeks could afford nothing but cheap local products. Then there's the problem of the debt- do they renege or print even more Drachmas to pay it. Same end result.

After first accepting the money, then reneging on every payment agreed upon, the Greeks are now demanding reparations from Germany for atrocities committed during WWII. (Giaginis, 2015)

These guys are wrong on so many levels as to be comical. These worthless, lazy, spendthrifts, if nothing else, have unmitigated gall.

If I were Germany, I would consider occupying them again! No one is condoning what happened in WWII, and maybe, just maybe, they may have been a bit too aggressive on occasions- but that's a story for another rant. Then again, war is hell. I don't approve of it in any way unless forced into it to protect one's own people. That being said, if boys must play at being men then I guess the point is to win.

Now, forget all that rant because the penultimate issue is that the reparations issue was laid to rest 25 years ago and the war has been over for 70 years. Gimme a break. This thing with picking and choosing a time in history that suits you and claiming something belongs to you because your great, great, great Gran pappy lost the old homestead somehow (probably because he got drunk and fell down a mine-shaft), therefore you should get it back. One might ask how come the issue didn't come up before Greece mooched off the Germans, (and the rest of the EU) in accepting their money to begin with. Bunch of crybabies looking for any way out of a predicament they caused themselves. Deflect the blame onto someone else and make them pay. Kinda reminds me of our legal system. A tactic as old as the hills, used by those in a bind- lash out, cornered rats and all that.

Finally, or primarily, it is beyond me why Germany puts up with these lazy SOB's in the first place. Really Angela, are those exports worth this kind of abuse? The Greeks are never going to pay anyway, just like the Argentinians. I guess if you admire hard work and living within your means it is logical to be pro German and anti-Greece. I'm sure Germany has its reasons for tolerating the Greeks

Tough break that the sun shines all year round in Greece (or any of many warm weather areas) so you don't feel the need or urge to do any work. Fine, don't work. But then you can't have all the pretty things that the Germans have. Because they went out into the cold and worked their rears off all their lives.

A day in the life of a Politician

What's it like? Part of the governmental process is the election of a President. Bill Clinton was committed to a balanced federal budget, moderately raised taxes only once, reformed welfare and signed the North American Free Trade Agreement (NAFTA), which seemed to be a good idea at the time.

Timing really is everything. Bill Clinton turned out to be fairly central and business-friendly. The economy was coming out of a recession when he entered office. Some say George Bush the elder really got the shaft on that one since it was really mostly his doing. Clinton mostly got out of the way- to his credit. If interest rates had already been low, energy prices high, the dollar weak and stock prices high, things might not have been so rosy for him. (Smith, 2015)

Hillary Clinton, during her first run for the presidency, claimed she would have opposed NAFTA, putting her in the cross hairs of the business community. (Catanese, 2014). All the storybooks say international free trade is extremely good for business and, hence, for profits. History does seem to bear that out so I can't be too quick to judge. Perhaps the problem is that the profits are all going to those at the top? The costs of a free trade policy are largely borne by the less-skilled workers of rich countries; its benefits flow largely to corporations. Hillary wanted to reverse the George Bush tax cuts, and favored increases in the Social Security tax for those at the top of the income scale. Opponents said all these measures tend to reduce both economic growth and investor returns. (Catanese)Says who and so what? Take a little less and have a more equitable and happy society. She also favors windfall taxes on oil companies (Catanese). Obama was, and is, more dovish on the Middle East, which may or may not be good policy. Is he pro-Arab because he is black? He is generally more trade-friendly. She proposed the gasoline-tax "holiday" during the 2008 primaries, to be paid for from the profits of big oil companies. Opponents said such a tax change would tend to increase oil consumption, driving up prices, worsening any global warming and benefiting largely the mega-wealthy oil states. Of the many silly time wasters like abortion and gay rights, this could be a discussion worth having.

CHAPTER TWELVE - SOLUTIONS

It's always amazing to see intelligent people clearly fall into two separate camps when considering how to deal with a broken economy that has expanded too fast and too much. One side believes in austerity, clean up your act, stop the speculation and drain all the excess from the system. It goes without saying that it would have been wise to never allow the speculation or expansion to occur in the first place. The other side feels that you must not let anyone suffer so print and lend your way out. Isn't it ironic that we ask the very people that caused the problem to fix it, and the solution to too much debt is more debt? You have to question whether the Fed simply can't control where their money goes, or they are just short sighted and corrupt by channeling it to the banks and the stock market and real estate.

Jim Puplava, says that "central banks can stimulate either production or employment or assets by printing money,." Unfortunately at the same time they "annihilate thrift, destroy morale and intellectual values and create the wealth disparity." (Puplava, 2005)

Everyone agrees that the longer you wait to make corrections the harder it is on everyone (except the rich and corrupt, of course). Those who disagree point to the Great Depression and incorrectly, in my view, say tightening the money supply is what caused it. I have discussed many time my feeling that the Depression was caused by the over indulgence of the

1920s and the loose credit attitude. Once you cause a boom it will sooner or later have to correct. The contraction in the 1930s was necessary. How much creating a war was a part of the overall plan to stimulate is suspect.

Here a few items to chew on. We have, poor tax incentives, poor government employees, ridiculous Congress and White House, greedy CEOs, and poorly thought out environmental policies that are much tougher than the competition, who took our jobs. Go ahead, show me your stuff. What would you do?

Maybe we should gear our efforts toward solutions rather than complaints. I believe the latter is called "Crisis Management."

So, what would be better?

INFLATION

Stop printing money! It punishes the savers, the elderly and those on a fixed income. Low interest only helps Governments pay off debts cheaply plus it forces savers to take risk for a decent return. Besides, Congress is lying about Social Security – It's my money- you just took it! Young people are putting money in for themselves, not me- I put mine in. The weak dollar only helps exports which is less than 15% of economy. A strong dollar would make imported goods cheaper. We do have a current account deficit, right? Stimulus is either entirely wrong because it reduces our dollar or is going to the wrong people or they are not passing it along as intended.

Balance the budget. Kick them out and/or jail them if they don't.

INEQUALITY

Stop Cronyism - Control the money going to the rich. It's not the incentive system of rewarding CEO's with stock options, it's the amount. Just make the options good after a long term track record has been established and make the options smaller. Stop the tax loopholes, stop the obscene perks and advantages. These measures also apply to actors, musicians, and sports figures. Pay all of them $300,000 per year tops. Reduce their obscene profits either up front or by taxes. The first time professional athletes check positive for steroids, they're banned for life and 90% of their money is confiscated.

The financial industry should be restructured entirely to limit pay and mandate what they are supposed to do- get money to where it does the most good.

Claw back money - from CEO's, Wall Street, Sports figures, old money and entertainers We need to go back several years, retrieving 75% of bonuses and payments. Or call it a one-time wealth tax.

While you are looking over the shoulder of the corporations insure that they don't pay overtime while laying off someone else. Overtime makes for a lousy family life anyway. The government does have to exercise some control or else the rich and powerful will run roughshod over you. The government needs to have a plan to assist corporations in capturing the expertise found in older workers before it is too late. Stop catering to slick talking youth who are shallow, don't have the work ethic, don't have the skills and are sick more. Besides, what's wrong with being paid for seniority? Reward kindness

WAR

The Military Industrial complex - Eliminate or control it! It's nothing but a war machine! Stop being a blustering bully. It's costly and makes enemies. If you're going to be a war monger at least get it right, attack Venezuela and take their oil. Why didn't we get any of Iraq's oil? I believe somebody forgot the rules for mercenaries. Charge for it! As to Iraq- seemed like we were damned if we do and damned if we don't- we liberated them and they couldn't wait to get us out. France also. We also need to stop standing up like the Redcoats and play by the same rules everyone else does. Think Vietnam, Iraq, Afghanistan, etc.

Get out and stay out of the Middle East. Reduce Globalization and reduce the size of the military. How can you not see through our war policy? First, we say we want nothing to do with the particular skirmish. Next we say we will only send in a few advisers. Then we increase the advisers to a few thousand. When that doesn't work we say we will do a few air strikes but no boots on the ground. Follow that up with a few troops to "support" the locals. Finally, the locals can't do the job so we will have to so we will systematically start send in troops, increasing them as needed according to the wishes of the Military Industrial machine. And usually by highly paid private contractors. Stay the hell out of other people's business.

Learn how to respond to Terrorism, after determining if there is any truth to their argument.

BANKS

Make them lend the money they were given on a silver platter.

Don't lend any more money to third world countries.

Stop Too big to fail. Congress gave billions of dollars to failing banks without any restrictions. The government also played right into their hands by taking away the incentive to lend- banks can put it right back in government securities with no risk. The banks are not honoring the agreement to get money into the economy, they are hoarding it to fatten their own balance sheets. Gave themselves big bonuses.

Reconsider Fractional banking.

GOVERNMENT

Create jobs! Increase wages for the average worker (take it from upper management).

Stop outsourcing -penalize the corporations that do it- a lot,and support a manufacturing effort with subsidies. Reduce the tax rate for companies in which the CEO's pay is no more than so many times that of a median employee. Even though it appears that Protectionism exacerbated the Great Depression, we cannot send our jobs overseas, especially if it has to do with manufacturing and we need it for war supplies-planes etc. Try Isolation again. No imports, no exports. When imports are allowed, there will be a 100% import tax on it. If you must outsource, have Chinese manufacturing units required to have an American partner. The American partner must get the tariff charged by the government. Get the shipping rights also. Keep the mills for training, marketing admin etc. Government, Universities and corporations must work together. Make sure those let go have education, severance and other job opportunities.

Fix Washington's attitude. Give them term limits and less perks and benefits- no lifetime pension for one term, and make them pay for their health insurance like the rest of us. Visit the entire lobbying system. It's the amount of compensation not the principle. The same medicine as should apply to CEOs should apply to all politicians. Every time you bet the farm, make sure their actual farm is in the mix also.

Welfare -Fix it and other government give away programs. They are necessary, just bloated and corrupted. It's too easy for the long term recipient to game the system. Stop paying fat mammas with 9 kids and 6'3" healthy men. After 1 illegitimate child no more free medical treatments, food stamps and welfare checks. You'll have to go to work. That means the government must insure there is a job for them. Welfare checks will be handed out on Fridays at the end of the 40 hour school week or infrastructure work week and the successful completion of urinalysis and a passing grade.

Social security will immediately be funded. Plus, if nothing in, nothing out. No politician can take from it.

Allow interest to go up- for Social Security, to increase Apartment Cap rates, and any other reliant calculation.

Minimum wage - Raise it or better still, reduce corporate and CEO obscene profits.

Immigration - Close the boarders. Stop catering to immigrants with special loans, education, and welfare. Speak English if you want to sell me something or live in my country.

Abortion (it's a woman's body) - What the hell does any government have to do with it?

Gay rights? - mind your own business!

EDUCATIONAL SYSTEM

Improve and cut the costs. When a mechanic or plumber or electrician earns as much (or more) as a college Professor, my guess is you're going to pay dearly down the road for that educational slight. Eliminate the fat here also and insure there are no poor teachers.

HEALTH CARE

Get smarter at spending. If not Obamacare, then do something, only do it right!

TECHNOLOGY

Funnel profits to everyone, not just the owners.

ENERGY   How about we peg oil prices to wheat or water? Or we could adapt a workable energy program. A little wind, solar, hydro, Biomass from throwaway parts of corn, switch-grass etc. I don't see too many starving gas station owners. I'm not sure about the actual gas price spread but I know they sure get their pound of flesh in mechanical work. Cap the oil company's profits or tax them more, or simply stop giving them so many incentives.   Revamp the Environment policy. Get less fanatical people. Tone down political correctness.

GUNS

There is no need to carry a weapon in order to hunt for food anymore. Are we a bunch of red neck macho bullies needing a fix, or do we need the guns to protect us from the bad guys?

PRISON SYSTEM - Revamp it. It should not be a for profit system. Let out the soft crime, non-violent offenders, cut off a few hands and kill the rest.

STOP WATCHING REALITY SHOWS - Consumers need to grow up and stop buying junk, especially from foreigners!

STOP SAYING "GOD BLESS AMERICA." It's great to have a God that believes in doing good works, taking care of others and the Golden Rule. I am not quite as impressed with your God when you insist that he is the only one and that I need to convert.

Yes, the entire world needs to be on board with fixes or money will just move across borders.

FURTHER RESEARCH

How long can a government perpetuate this printing of money?

Before we were a consumption economy how did we manage?

Could money printing have helped previous depressions or recessions such as the Great Depression?

Why must we expand or die?

APPENDIX A COMPREHENSIVE PLAN TO BALANCE THE BUDGET

Area	Potential Savings
CORPORATE TAXES	**$150 BILLION**

TAXES @ 90% if firm received funds from Govt

TALANT PAY-   **$250 BILLION**

Place a huge surtax (entertainment) or cap on non essential professions, e.g., actors, musicians, sports figures. Tax the entertainer, not the purchaser of the ticket! Paying a fat illiterate slob to play football 5 mil a year to grunt, and a concert pianist $100k. Something is wrong with this picture. Assume 200 actors, 200 musicians, 200 baseball, Football (assume 30 teams x 30 players=1000 x 2 mil= $2 Billion, Basketball -same, or 5000 people making $20 million each = $10 billion at a 60% tax rate

PROGRESSIVE TAX   **$350 BILLION**

500 Billionaires earn $2 billion/yr on average or $1 trillion. @ 70% tax that equals $700 billion – even if half its $350 billion 350 CEO's make $20 mil or 7 billion so, 50% tax= $3.5 billion. Even if it doesn't make a dent in the debt it should be done for fairness and to make average people feel the rich are doing their part – way low!!!!!

200,000 millionaires earn average of $2 million. Tax @ 50%= 1 million ea. Or Alt min tax on assets???

$200 BILLION

How can we tax the permanent rich trust type income yet encourage savings?

Maybe a one-time tax also?

Limit tax deductions to 15%-   **$141 BILLION**

Eliminate loopholes in tax deductions unless increasing plants or production or training people etc.

All forms of personal income to be taxed all the way, even beyond one million dollars as well as interest, dividends and unearned income. SS and Medicare to be taxed all the way even though the rich don't need it and shouldn't get it. Treat it like a sales tax only on what you earned. Place a tax of 1/10 of 1% on every purchase of a financial instrument. No taxes on anyone making under $40,000

ALLOW TAX CUTS TO EXPIRE $276 BILLION

The tax breaks of 2008 or 9 were supposed to be temporary- so it's just another political commitment the republicans never intended to honor.

RAISE SS PAYROLL TAX CAP ALL THE WAY!
FUND IT/DON'T TOUCH $66 BILLION

Remember: this is not an entitlement! We contributed to the fund and the government was not supposed to touch that money, but invest it.

MERCENARY FEES – if you must be a bully, at least get paid for it   **$200 BILLION**

LAW SUIT TAX $200 BILLION
after so much 1/2% of 5 trillion. Punish offenders but limit lawyers and plaintiffs. Give rest to a fund for the poor or infrastructure. Make tax code simpler and stop changing it so often

WALL STREET TRADING $75 BILLION
Simply place a tax of ½ of 1% on every purchase of a financial instrument. Assume $30 Trillion a year. Take 50% of that, so we have 15 Trillion to tax @ .5%
TARIFFS – for outsourcing and importing and downsizing. Incentives for not outsourcing ????????

SAVINGS/OLD MONEY TAX- 15% AFTER A MINIMUM 6 BILLION
30 families @ 1 bil, 100 @ 100 mil

NATIONAL SALES TAX $345 BILLION
more for luxury items

RAISE PART B MEDICARE PREMIUMS 10%
20 BILLION

SUV – GAS GUZZLER TAX ??????
Sub Total Revenue saved-**$2.3 TRILLION**
OR- alternatively

INDIVIDUAL TAX - $50k x 120 mil workers @ 20%
1.2 Trillion
CORPORATE TAX at 20% **4.2 trillion**

Top 100	1.4 Trillion
Top 100-200	383 bil
Top 200-300	213 bil
Top 300-400	144 bil
Top 400-500	106 bil

OR alternatively

GDP @ 16 trillion x .15 flat tax =   **2 Trillion**

CUT MILITARY 20%   **140 billion**

600 billion in 2009,700 bil-2011

Efficiency initiatives -military	28 bil
Replace F35 with F16, F18	4.5 bil
Cut Troops in Europe	100 bil

They hate us anyway.

80mil -Europe, 50mil-Japan, 30mil-Korea

Iraq/Afgan wars/occupation	113bil

CUT ALL GOVT BUDGET BY 15%   220bil

Waste and overhead, salaries in line, cut congressional and white House budget and perks-

Free mail(100mil), first class air(100mil) 4.4 mil people/buildings/supplies

Reduce Presidential travel expenses	1 bil
Cut Congressional pensions	30 bil
Eliminate earmarks	16 bil
Freeze hiring	13bil
Reduce contract employees	18 bil
Freeze pay for GS ratings for 3 years	6bil
Farm subsidies + all ag (140 bil	30 bil

Oil Subsidies	30 bil
Education Dept	50 bil
Health Ed. and Welfare	**20 bil**

Oil - Stop importing   **750 bil**

But at least it would stay in the US and avoid going to places that hate us. Have the government buy bulk and store it. Raise the price of food sent there and store the spread in profits. Oil Imports are $331 billion per year (at $90/bbl) out of GDP of 14 Trillion- 6 Bil x 75% x $75/barrel. This figure goes to 700 billion at $140/barrel.

REDUCE FOREIGN AID 40%- Isolationism? Don't bribe a rogue nation. Speak softly and carry a big stick. Warn them, plead with them. Then bomb them into oblivion. Stay out of Civil Wars. Restrict nuclear arms in

hostile countries. PROBLEM. Government lends money to Country A who buys U.S. Business exports. Ergo, that one U.S. Business gets rich. Country A can't produce well enough to pay their debts, but they can produce well enough to undercut our other businesses? We pay more in taxes for the bad debt and the money isn't available for other things. Train staff working overseas in local cultures, languages and courtesy for a better reputation and better lines of communication. Concentrate on the little projects that help the average person in the lesser developing countries.   **18 billion**

ELIMINATE UNITED NATIONS 3.6 billion
Don't participate and remove them from our country.

IMMIGRATION - Eliminate costs such as free education and health and welfare. They don't pay taxes. Close the boarder, build the wall, we are still better than Europe. You can't even get work in Europe if you are not a member of the EU. Americans will work the job if it paid better. No amnesty

PROTECTIONISM-No imports if we can mfg it "the 'free trade crowd doesn't get it, but the steel worker in Allentown, Penna. who is now a bagger at Walmart understands." Adapt a clear and enforceable "Level Field" policy on trade. Exempt those items that relate to national security and infant industries. As long as we believe there's a possibility of a conventional ground war we should be reinforcing our basic manufacturing capabilities; Steel, Farming, Textiles, Rubber, Plastics and Energy. However, if someone does it cheaper, maybe find a way to use them on a piece meal basis, still maintain control of critical technology and spend the profit spread on training. Tariffs should go partially to corporations and to workers in corporations and some to government. Subsidize good companies also. Twenty years ago the Democrats lost elections because of NAFTA. The Republicans don't want you to know that the tainted strawberries came from Mexico. The Republicans don't want you to know that Walmart FORCED that shirt manufacturer to move to China. The Republicans think that replacing American steel with foreign steel is good for America. The Republicans want us to compete with prison labor. The

US opens the world to "free trade," and then loses market share. It celebrates its own superiority, while the whole world laughs at it." Our wages will eventually fall, even as the Chinese increase theirs. But even if their wages are the same, our quality isn't there so we will still not be able to sell products.

OVERHAUL WELFARE- require education classes. Pick up check after work on infrastructure, etc. Those in good health need not apply. Something like the Civilian Conservation Corps (CCC), a New Deal public works program.

ELIMINATE STATE AND LOCAL DEDUCTIONS		**94 billion**
MEDICARE	2011	**120 billion**
SOCIAL SECURITY	2011	**120 billion**

Both these programs are supposed to be self funding- the Govt spent the money that was to be drawing interest

EPA – revamp – drill for oil yet protect environment. Doesn't matter about the spotted owl if you can't afford food.

Sub Total Cuts	**1.7 Trillion**
Total	**4.0 Trillion**

That's now! Not over 10 years

SPENDING NEEDED

Car Manufacturing – If you must use them, then build
        them here. It would provide jobs and a tax base.
Health Care – Make it better and less expensive. Fund
Medicare! Poor health care system and expensive due to
high cost of medical school debt, E&O insurance for
malpractice, our expensive way of life and sheer greed.
No health insurance for 45mil people. But, Europe has
not been number one for years and they manage better
social medicine
Create Jobs!
Manufacturing – subsidize - hedge fund use of funds is
not a productive use- should be building factories to
produce steel, clothing, batteries,exploring for minerals,
farming, research-alt energy. Losing manufacturing-
what if a war? Support with tax credits and grants to
companies like Costco- their CEO makes $500,000,
employees make $17/hr and get good benefits. (2013)
Minimum wage-for citizens, $12-15/hour
Make the unemployed work on public projects. Henry
Ford raised salaries to $5 per day so people could afford
his cars. It worked. Walmart should raise salaries here,
pay a little more for American materials, or go out of
business altogether, so people here could have jobs- the
people would then be willing to pay a little more.
Education   in the work force, for those who are
unemployed or underemployed and to the children.
Work training programs- apprentice programs (WPA or
CCC)- will create better jobs. Free education- Provide
more education slots to eliminate discrimination, not put

in place of a better qualified person. Better teacher pay-
only in line with public. Better schools

Concentrate on eliminating the single parent home with
training and moral value adjustment in our culture.
Punish troublemakers in schools and welfare- (already
77 billion)

Alt Energy Grants -shale oil production, coal
production/conversion, natural gas

Subsidize industry-steel, airplane, farming,
hydro, hydrogen,

Give tax credits or grants- especially within the
boarders – see oil above 750 billion

Infrastructure – we can't do it because we have no money

Social Security – Fund it!

Lending- 2nd wave of foreclosures and commercial
foreclosures, leverage of derivatives. Banks are hiding
bad loans with modifications. Bailouts of Financials-
will cause inflation. Banks not lending! Consumers- cut
loan amount to current market value, give a 90% loan
on that at 4%- to instill some incentive to continue to
pay maybe concede to take it to 100% as a punishment
for their part in this mess. Lenders- limit loss they must
take to 30% (or whatever) possibly share the losses
with Wall Street (now only a 15% loss). Wall Street
eat 30% also. Investors (who bought the securitized
paper) eat some. Bondholders especially Government
eats the rest. No pork added to these bills.

They do what you tell them to do or close them
down. If they go offshore, have all the depositors pull
their money out and start a new local bank. Even if it
was just a mistake or stupid, they should not be

allowed to be bailed out or get bonuses-especially if they were bailed out.. Stockholders should lose all and management should be fired. There is always someone waiting in the wings to take over and run the bank- so how could the system crash?

GLOSSSARY

Animal Spirits Theory: People, acting out of emotion, do irrational things. Could be the opposite of the Efficient Market Theory (EMT) or at least why the EMT isn't true.

Austrian Business Cycle: Inflation sets off the business cycle. Austrian economists hold this to be the most damaging effect of inflation. According to Austrian theory, artificially low interest rates and the associated increase in the money supply lead to reckless speculative borrowing, resulting in clusters of mal-investments, which eventually have to be liquidated as they become unsustainable.

Bear Market- A downward trend in the stock market. The generally accepted measure is 20% over a two month period.

Black Swan: an unusual, unforeseen event one could not have seen coming.

Boondoggle: considered a useless waste of both time and money, yet often continued anyway in spite of good sense saying otherwise.

Bull Market - a period of generally rising prices in the stock market. A trend upwards.

Commercial Paper an unsecured or un-backed money-market security issued (sold) by large corporations to obtain funds to meet short-term debt obligations.

Comparative Advantage: The ability of a party to produce a particular good or service at a lower margin and opportunity cost. Even if one country is more efficient in the production of all goods than another, both countries will still gain by trading with each other.

Currency Board: Every unit of the domestic currency is backed by a corresponding number of units of dollars or other foreign currencies in the central bank's vault.

Deflation: A decrease in the prices of goods and services, usually tied to a contraction of money in circulation.

Demonetize: To stop using, take from circulation, divest a currency of its value.

Depression: A recession where the peak-to-trough (highest to lowest point) contraction in real growth exceeds 10%.

GDP (Goss Domenstic Production): all the goods and services produced *by a nation*

General Equilibrium Theory: Studies supply and demand fundamentals in an economy with multiple markets, with the objective of proving that a set of prices exists that will result in an overall equilibrium. Credit stems from the 1870s and Leon Walrus.

Giffen Paradox: According to the Law of Demand, when the price of a commodity falls the demand for it rises. Giffen's Paradox is an exception to the Law of Demand. A rise in the price of bread makes so large a drain on the resources of the poorer laboring families that they are forced to curtail their consumption of meat and other expensive items. They consume more bread, since it is still the cheapest food, and not less of it.

Great Depression: A depression where the peak-to-trough contraction in real growth exceeds 25%.

Hyperinflation: A cumulative inflation rate minimally in excess of four-digit annual percent change, where the involved currency becomes worthless, and people know it and don't want it. Crudely put, it's when "it's not worth the paper it's printed on." It is extremely rapid, or out of control, inflation. Hyperinflation is often associated with wars, economic depressions, and political or social upheavals. *However!* In both classical economics and monetarism, it is always the result of the monetary authority irresponsibly borrowing money to pay all its expenses."

IMF -International Monetary Fund -
Inflation: a rise in the general level of prices so your currency buys fewer goods and services. Your money

has less purchasing power   (a loss of currency's value).

A different viewpoint is that the above is only the result of inflation. Inflation is strictly money printing, which causes a rise in the general level of prices. It is not the result, which includes increased prices and wages.

Inverted Yield Curve: When the difference in interest rates between the short and long terms narrows, the yield curve flattens. When long-term rates fall below short-term rates, you get the inverted yield curve. That means you have achieved the absurd condition where you are getting paid less money for loaning your money for a longer term, and at higher risk! (Richard Daughty, 2005).

Kondratiev's Economic Cycle Theory: Held that there were long cycles of about fifty years. At first, economies produce high cost capital goods and infrastructure investments creating new employment, income, and a demand for consumer goods. After a few decades overcapacity gives rise to layoffs, reducing the demand for consumer goods. Unemployment and a long economic crisis ensue as economies contract. People and companies save their resources until confidence begins to return and the process starts over, usually initiated by new technologies.

Labor Theory of Value: aka the cost-of-production theory of value, states that the value of an object is the cost to make it including labor, capital, land, or technology.

Marginal Theory of Value (1870s) to have value an object must be both useful and scarce to a consumer as opposed to the cost of production theory of value believed by classical economists.

Marshall Plan (officially the European Recovery Program, ERP) was an American initiative to aid Europe and Asia, in which the United States gave $13 billion (approximately $120 billion in current dollar value) in economic support to help rebuild European economies after the end of World War II. Proposed and named after then United States Secretary of State, General George C. Marshall.

Non-Accelerating Inflation Rate of Unemployment (NAIRU): A level of unemployment you can have without having inflation.

Quantitative Easing: A government monetary policy used to increase the money supply by buying government securities or other securities from the market. QE increases the money supply by flooding financial institutions with capital, in an effort to promote increased lending and liquidity.

Quantity Theory of Money: When the supply of money goes up the price (value) comes down. Print money and value reduces.

Recession: Two or more consecutive quarters of contracting real (inflation-adjusted) GDP, where the downturn is not triggered by any outlier factor, or Black Swan (these are events that cannot be foreseen), like anything they can use as an excuse to not call it a recession.

SDR: Special Drawing Rights - An international type of monetary reserve currency, created by the International Monetary Fund (IMF) in 1969, which operates as a supplement to the existing reserves of member countries. Created in response to concerns about the limitations of gold and dollars as the sole means of settling international accounts, SDRs are designed to augment international liquidity by supplementing the standard reserve currencies. The currency value of the SDR is determined by summing the values in U.S. dollars, based on market exchange rates, of a basket of major currencies (the U.S. dollar, Euro, Japanese yen, and pound sterling).

Seigniorage: The difference between the value of money and the cost to produce and distribute goods and services.

Specie: In kind, as in distribution in kind (Specie). It occurs when a company pays a dividend in stock, rather than in cash or pays back a loan in gold rather than cash. It has evolved to mean a form of hard asset (like metal) rather than a depreciating asset. The phrase "in specie" is Latin for "in its actual form". Real value rather than "Fiat", paper currency.

Sticky Prices: When other things change, like supply or demand, it takes prices longer to change.

The Velocity of Money: A larger number of transactions or faster movement of money (each piece of money is used more often), so it's like more money. Hyperinflation panics do this. It can be a vicious circle. The good news, if any, is it's a rare occurrence.

Too Big To Fail: An economic theory stating that certain banks (and other entities) are too intertwined in, and have too much effect on, the overall economy and therefore should get preferential treatment and not be allowed to fail because the result would be too much to bear for the economy.

REFERENCES

Amadeo, K. (2015). *National Debt by Years, compared by GDP and major events.* useconomy.

Amoss, D. (2009). *This Stock Market is rented, not Owned.* Agora Publishing.

Andrews, E. (2014). *8 Things You Should Know About WWII's Eastern Front.* history.com.

Arends, B. (2010). *Th Three Biggest Lies about the U.S. Economy.* Marketwatch.

Batra, R. (1987). *The Great Depression of 1990.* Simon & Schuster.

Bendery, J. (2014). *Spend More On Defense, Not On Roads Or Food Stamps.* Huffington Post.

Benedict, P., & Gutmann, M. (2005). *Early Modern Europe: From Crisis to Stability.* University of Delaware Press.

Blumen, R. (2005). *Bernankiasm, Menace or Fraud?* lewrockwell.com.

Boeree, G. (2006). *Personality Theories.* ebook-self published.

Bonner, B. (2006). *Empire of Debt.* Agora Publishing.

Bonner, B. (2006). *The Hyper-inflationary Depression.* Agora.

Bonner, B. (2011). *Here is our most audacious forecast yet.* Agora Publishing.

Bonner, B. (2014). *Hormegeddon: How Too Much of a Good Thing Leads to Disaster.* Lioncrest.

Bonner, B. (2014). *Poor Ron Paul.* Agora Publishing.

Brodick, S. (2008). *Oil Crisis Worsening, what next.....* Money and markets.

Bullard, J. (2010). *Three Lesson from the Monetary Panic of 2008.* Federal Reserve Bank of St. Louis.

Cannan, E. (1931). *Modern Currency and the Regulation of Its Value.* P.S.King.

Carlson, D. (2014). *Collapse of oil prices leads world economy into trouble.* The Guardian.

Catanese, D. (2014). *What Would Hillary Do?* US News.

Charles, D. (2008). *What We Can Learn from Hamilton & Another "Bail Out".* Historynewsnetwork.org.

Constitution Of The Union Of Soviet Socialist Republics. (1977). Bucknell University Press.

Crutsinger, M. (2015). *US unemployment rise attributed to temporary auto plant shutdowns.* The Associated Press.

Dalio, R. (2015). *How the Economic Machine Works .* Economic Principles.

Davidson, A. (2012). *The Real Reason Gas costs $4 per Gallon.* NPR.

Dent, H. (2014). *The 2 Reasons Why the Aussie Dollar is Done For.* economyandmarkets.

Dent, H. (2015). *China's Economic Spiral.* Economy and Markets.

Derber, C. (2000). *The Pursuit of Attention: Power and Ego in Everyday Life.* Oxford University Press.

Desilver, D. (2014). *For most workers, real wages have barely budged for decades.* Pew Research.

Dickinson, T. (2014). *The Biggest Tax Scam Ever.* Rolling Stone.

Douglas, F. (2015). *Quotes.* http://thinkexist.com/.

Dudwa, P. D. (2015). *Chronic Inflation causes and burden.* mwnation.

Durden, T. (2013). *9 Signs that China is making a move against the dollar.* Zerohedge.

Durden, T. (2014). *21 Facts That Prove That Government Dependence Is Out Of Control In America.* Zero Hedge.

Durden, T. (2014a). *A List Of 97 Taxes Americans Pay Every Year.* zerohedge.

Ehrenberg, R., Danziger, L., & San, G. (1983). *Cost of Living Adjustment Clauses in Union Contracts.* Cornell University Press.

Encyclopedia Britannica. (2015). *Assignats-French.* Encyclopedia Britannica.

Esposito, J., & Mogahed, D. (2007). *Who Speaks for Islam? What a Billion Muslims Really Think.* Gallup Press.

Federal Reserve Board of San Francisco. (2009). *How has the percentage of consumer debt compared to household income changed over the last few decades? What is driving these changes?* Federal Reserve board.

Fehér, F. e. (1990). *The French Revolution and the Birth of Modernity.* University of California Press Berkeley.

Fischer, S., & Modigliani, F. (1978). *Towards An Understanding of the Real Effects and Costs of Inflation.* National Bureau of Economic Research.

Fisher, D. (1996). *The Great Wave.* Oxford Univ. Press.

Fraser, D. (2012). *Burning issues for the world's future.* BBC.

French, D. (2014). *The Morality Test: Capitalism vs Government.* Casey Daily Research.

Friedman, T. (2005). *It's a Flat World After All.* NYTimes.

Friedman, T. (2005). *It's a Flat world Afterall.* New York Times.

Giaginis, L. (2015). *Greece's Clain for War Reparations from Germany Explained.* Euronews.

Giles, D. (2014). *What are the Odds IRS comedy hour in which seven hard drives crashed at the same time and a simple "sorry" got them out of any responsibility. The expression What are the odds of 7 hard drives crashing in the same month?* ClashDaily.

Goldberg, J. (2015). *Connecting the Dots Between Greek Crisis, Argentina — and the 'Shylock' Canard.* Forward.

Goldstone, J. (1991). *Revolution and Rebellion in the Early Modern World.* University of California Press.

Greider, W. (2005). *America's True Deficit.* www.skeptically.org.

Griffin, G. E. (1994). *The Creature from Jekyll Island* . American Opinion Publishing.

Grim, R. (2010). *Alan Simpson: Social Security Is 'A Milk Cow With 310 Million Tits.* Huffington Post.

Hamid, T. (2014). *Energy forecast.* J.P.Morgan.

Hanlon, M. (2014). *The golden quarter.* Aeon.

Hardcastle, E. (1990). *Inflation: The Endless farce.* www.marxists.org.

Hogarth, J. M., Anguelov, C. E., & Lee, J. (2004). *Why Don't Households Have a Checking Account?.* Journal of Consumer Affairs.

Hoisington, V., & Hunt, L. (2014). *Quarterly Review and Outlook Fourth Quarter 2013.* Outside the Box: Hoisington Investment Management:.

IndexMundi. (2014). *Oil Consumption per Capita.* IndexMundi.

Investopedia. (1996). *definition-hetroskedasticity.* investopedia.

Isidore, C. (2005). *GM to Cut 25,000 Jobs by '08.* CNN.

Jefferson, T. (1798). *The Founders' Constitution-Resolutions Relative to the Alien and Sedition Acts.* press-pubs@uchicago.edu.

Kelly, M. (2015). *The Top 5 Causes That Led to World War I.* americanhistory.about.com.

King, J. (2014). *Propaganda and Islam: What you're not Being Told.* Antimedia.

Klinger, S., Anderson, S., & Rojas, J. (2014). *Corporate Tax Dodgers.* Institute for Policy Studies.

Koepka, H. (2014). *America Is NOT The Greatest Country Anymore! - Jeff Daniels/HBO-Newsroom.* HBO.

Krist, B. (2014). *Did the Smoot-Hawley Tariff Cause the Great Depression?* Washington International Trade Association.

Krugman, P. (2015). *The Rage of Bankers.* New york Times.

Krugman, P. (2015b). *Dewey, Cheatem & Howe.* New York Times.

Krugman, P. (2015c). *Republicans Against Retirement.* New York Times.

Labissoniere, M., & Bowe, S. (2005). *Estimating the impact of foreign competition on the Wisconsin wood furniture industry. Part 1 A quantitative input-output analysis.* Forest Products Society.

LeBeau, P. (2012). *Manufacturers Pay a Bounty for Skilled Workers.* CNBC.

Lee, D., & Douglass, E. (2005). *Chinese Drop Takeover Bid for Unocal.* LA Times.

Lewis, M. (2011). *It's the Economy, Dummkopf.* Vanity Fair.

Lewis-Beck, M., & Stegmaier, M. (2007). *Economic Models of Voting.* Oxford University Press.

Lowe, C. (2014). *Who Will blink First in the Oil Wars?* Bonnerandpartners.

Lowenstein, R. (2001). *When Genius Failed: The Rise and Fall of Long-Term Capital Management.* Random House.

Madison, J. (1787). Speech at the Constitutional Convention. *Constitutional Convention.* James Madison.

Marx, K. (1867). *Das Capital, A Critique of Political Economy. Friedrich Engels (ed).* Regnery Publishing 1996.

Mattox, J. M. (2006). *Saint Augustine and the Theory of Just War.* Continuum.

Mauldin, J. (2006). *A Congressional Tantrum.* Agora Publishing.

Mayer, C. (2005). *What Red Menace?* Agora Publishing.

McClosky, D. N. (2010). *The Bourgeois Virtues: Ethics for an Age of Commerce.* University of Chicago Press.

McCullagh, D. (2010). *Intel CEO: U.S. faces looming tech decline.* CNET.

McLoad, S. (2007). *Maslow's Hierarchy of Needs.* Simple Psychology.

Mickey, A. (2007). *OPEC's Continued Irrelevance.* BreakAwayInvestor.

Miller, C. (2014). *Why the U.S. Has Fallen Behind in Internet Speed and Affordability.* New York Times.

Milne, S. (2014). *It's not Russia that's pushed Ukraine to the brink of war.* The Guardian.

Minsky, h. (2008). *Stabilizing an Unstable Economy.* Yale University Press.

Moen, J., & Tallman, E. W. (1992). *The Bank Panic of 1907: The Role of the Trust Companies.* Journel of Economic History.

Moen, J., & Tallman, E. W. (2000). *Clearinghouse Membership and Deposit Contraction during the Panic of 1907.* Journel of Economic History.

Morrison, P. (2015). *Not an Islam I can recognize, a Muslim scholar discusses the Paris attacks.* LATimes.

National Academy of Engineers. (2008). *The Offshoring of Engineering: Facts, Unknowns, and Potential Implications.* National Academy Press.

New World Encyclopedia. (2015). *Operation Barbarosa.* New World Encyclopedia.

Organization of Economic Cooperation and Development . (2012). *Level of GDP per Capita and Productivity.* OECD.

Osterberg, W. P., & Thomson, J. B. (1998). Bank Notes and Stored-Value Cards: Stepping Lightly into the Past. *Economic Commentary-Cleveland.*

Perkins, R. (2013). *US-led shale boom no long-term threat for OPEC'S oil - IEA.* Platts.

Persaud, A. (1995). *Before and Beyond EMU: Historical Lessons and Future Prospects.* Routledge.

Peterson, P. (2004). *Running on Empty: How the Democratic and Republican Parties Are Bankrupting Our Future and What Americans Can Do About It.* Farrar, Straus and Giroux.

Piketty, T. (2014). *Capital in the 21st Century.* Harvard University Press.

Powell, J. (1996). *William Ewart Gladstone's Campaign for Peace and Freedom.* Foundation for Economic Education.

Puplava, J. (2005). *The core Rate.* Financial Sense.

Reeves, J. (2012). *17 Frightening Facts About Retirement Savings in America.* theMotleyFool.

Reinhart, C., Reinhart, V. R., & Rogoff, K. (2012). *Reinhart, Carmen M., Reinhart, Vincent R. and Rogoff, Kenneth S. (2012). Public Debt Overhangs: Public Debt Overhangs: Advanced-Economy Episodes Since 1800, .* Journal of Economic Perspectives, Volume 26.

Roosevelt, F. D. (1938). *Public Papers and Addresses of Franklin D. Roosevelt, Volumne II, ears of Crisis.* Random House.

Rosenburg, P. (2014). *They Walk Among Us.* A Free Man's Take.

Rostand, J. (1938). *Thoughts of a Biologis.* Littlefield Book ServiceLtd.

Rothbard, M. (1963). *America's Great Depression.* John Van Nostrand.

Rummel, R. (1994). *Death by Government.* Transaction Publishers.

Sachs, J. (2006). *The Social Welfare State, beyond Ideology.* Scientific American.

Schumpeter, J. (1942). *Capitalism, Socialism and Democracy.* Harper & Row.

Shenoy, S. (2009). *A Tiger By the Tail: The Keynesian Legacy of Inflation by F.A. Hayek.* Ludwig von Mises Institute.

Smith, Y. (2015). *15 Ways Bill Clinton's White House Failed America.* Naked Capitalism.

Sorkin, A. R. (2010). *Too Big to Fail: The Inside Story of How Wall Street and Washington Fought ...* Penguin Books.

Spencer, R. (2008). *The Politically Incorrect Guide to Islam (and the Crusades).* Regnery Publishing.

Sprague, O. M. (1910). *History of Crises under the National Banking System.* National Monetary Commission. Washington, D.C.:U.S. Government Printing Office.

Suderman, P. (2014). *The U.S. Military Budget Is Bigger Than the 10 Next Biggest Military Budgets Combined.* Reason.com.

Tax Foundation. (2013). *U.S. Federal Individual Income Tax Rate History.* taxfoundation.org.

Thomas, H. (2007). *Roubini's verdict – this is worse than LTCM.* Financial times.

Tier, M. (2005). *An American Ultimatum.* Agora.

TSK News. (2009). *News fro Yahoo.Finance.* Yahoo.Finance.

U.S. Bureau of Labor Statistics. . (2015). *CPI Inflation Calculator.* Government Printing Office.

U.S. Treasury. (2016). *US NATIONAL DEBT BY YEAR.* government Printing Office.

U.S.State Department. (2015). *The Iranian Hostage Crisis.* Bureau of Public Affairs.

Watts, A. (2009). *Ike's second warning, hint: it is not the "military-industrial complex.* What's up with that?

Weiss, M. (2009). *The Ultimate Depression Survival Guide.* John Wiley & Sons.

Weiss, M. (2009a). *Dangerous Unintended consequences.* Moneyandmarkets.

Werner, R. (2015). *A lost century in economics: Three theories of banking and the conclusive evidence.* International Review of financial Analysis.

Williams, J. (2013). *UInemployment Rates.* Shadow Statistics.

Wofford, T. (2014). *Dick Cheney:I Have no Regrets About the Iraq War.* Newsweek.

Woodford, M. (2010). *Simple Analytics of the Government Expenditure Multiplier, (The Zero Lower Bound Problem).* macroeconomic analysis.com.

World Bank. (2012). *Poverty Overview.* World Bank.

Yardini, E., & Johnson, D. (2015). *US Economic Indicators: Corporate Profits in GDP .* Yardini Research.

Zinn, H. (1980). *A People's History of the USA, .* Harper & Row: Harper Collins.

www.ingramcontent.com/pod-product-compliance
Lightning Source LLC
Chambersburg PA
CBHW060324200326
41519CB00011BA/1825